Congressional Research Service

Proliferation Control Regimes: Background and Status

Mary Beth Nikitin, Coordinator
Analyst in Nonproliferation

Paul K. Kerr
Analyst in Nonproliferation

Steven A. Hildreth
Specialist in Missile Defense

October 18, 2010

Congressional Research Service

7-5700

www.crs.gov

RL31559

CRS Report for Congress ———————

Prepared for Members and Committees of Congress

Summary

Weapons of mass destruction (WMD), especially in the hands of radical states and terrorists, represent a major threat to U.S. national security interests. Multilateral regimes were established to restrict trade in nuclear, chemical, and biological weapons and missile technologies, and to monitor their civil applications. Congress may consider the efficacy of these regimes in considering the potential renewal of the Export Administration Act, as well as other proliferation-specific legislation in the 111th Congress. This report provides background and current status information on the regimes.

The nuclear nonproliferation regime encompasses several treaties, extensive multilateral and bilateral diplomatic agreements, multilateral organizations and domestic agencies, and the domestic laws of participating countries. Since the dawn of the nuclear age, U.S. leadership has been crucial in developing the regime. While there is almost universal international agreement opposing the further spread of nuclear weapons, several challenges to the regime have arisen in recent years: India and Pakistan tested nuclear weapons in 1998, North Korea withdrew from the Nuclear Nonproliferation Treaty (NPT) in 2003 and tested a nuclear explosive device in 2006 and 2009, Libya gave up a clandestine nuclear weapons program in 2004, and Iran was found to be in non-compliance with its treaty obligations in 2005. The discovery of the nuclear black market network run by A.Q. Khan spurred new thinking about how to strengthen the regime, including greater restrictions on sensitive technology. However, the extension of civil nuclear cooperation by the United States and other countries to India, a non-party to the NPT with nuclear weapons, has raised questions about what benefits still exist for non-nuclear-weapons states that remain in the treaty regime.

The chemical and biological weapons (CBW) nonproliferation regimes contain three elements: the Chemical Weapons Convention (CWC), the Biological and Toxin Weapons Convention (BWC), and the Australia Group. The informal Australia Group coordinates export controls on CBW-related materials and technology. After 25 years of negotiations, the CWC entered into force in April 1997. It prohibits the development, production, stockpiling, transfer, and use of chemical weapons, and mandates the destruction of existing chemical weapon arsenals. Since its 1972 inception, BWC state parties have failed to agree on a verification mechanism.

The missile nonproliferation regime is founded not on a treaty, but an informal agreement created in 1987, the Missile Technology Control Regime (MTCR). The MTCR's goal is to limit the spread of missiles capable of carrying nuclear weapons. Thirty-four countries now adhere to the guidelines, which have been modified over time to include missile systems designed for the delivery of chemical and biological weapons. The regime, which has no enforcement organization, is thought to have been instrumental in blocking several missile programs, but it has been unable to stop North Korean missile development, production, and exports, or to win the full cooperation of Russian and Chinese entities. This report is updated annually.

Contents

Tables

Appendixes

Contacts

Introduction

The United States has historically led the international community in establishing regimes intended to limit the spread of nuclear, chemical, and biological weapons and missiles. The regimes and their member countries use cooperative and coercive measures to achieve nonproliferation and counterproliferation objectives. Multilateral agreements and organizations are supplemented by strong bilateral cooperation among key allies, unilateral political and economic actions, and recourse to military operations should they become necessary. Congress supports the nonproliferation regimes primarily by providing statutory authority and funding for U.S. participation, establishing policy, and mandating punitive actions to help enforce the international standards set by the regimes.

The term "regime" often refers to the entire array of international agreements, multilateral organizations, national laws, regulations, and policies to prevent the spread of dangerous weapons and technologies. The nuclear nonproliferation regime is presently the most extensive, followed by those dealing with chemical and biological weapons, and then by the missile regime. The difficulty of producing nuclear weapons material (highly enriched uranium or plutonium) and the great awareness of nuclear weapons' destructiveness together have been conducive to creating a complex regime with widespread agreement on the priority of nuclear nonproliferation. Chemical weapons are easier to make and rely on readily available precursors, and they are far less destructive. Biological weapons also rely on dual-use technology, and as technology has spread, efforts to build a more extensive control regime have intensified. Finally, there is no international consensus on the danger of missile proliferation to support a nonproliferation treaty or a binding regime with enforcement mechanisms.

A key aspect of all the regimes is their attempt to control exports of sensitive goods and technologies through supplier agreements. These are the Nuclear Suppliers Group and the Zangger Committee for nuclear technology, the Australia Group for chemical and biological weapons technology, and the Missile Technology Control Regime. In the last decade, these export control regimes have expanded their membership, expanded and refined their control lists, and increased coordination among member states. At the same time, however, the non-binding nature of some of the regimes and growing resistance to them by certain countries, including some regime members, limits their effectiveness. A major dilemma is whether to include new members, that may not be U.S. allies and may not have reliable export controls, or to limit membership to countries with excellent nonproliferation credentials. Regime members are afforded special access to controlled technology by the other members, so this issue also affects decisions on whether to include non-allies. **Table 1** lists the proliferation control regimes, their components and statutory authority. There are many arms control treaties and other activities that address aspects of WMD and conventional weapons beyond the regimes covered in this report.[1]

Status and Trends

Although proliferation control regimes are a useful tool in preventing dangerous technology transfers, several factors undermine their effectiveness. One is the difficulty of addressing underlying motivations of countries to acquire weapons of mass destruction (WMD). Regional

---

[1] See also CRS Report RL33865, *Arms Control and Nonproliferation: A Catalog of Treaties and Agreements*, by Amy F. Woolf, Mary Beth Nikitin, and Paul K. Kerr

security conditions as well as the desire to compensate for other countries' superior conventional or unconventional forces have been common motivations for WMD programs. Some countries may want WMD to dominate their adversaries. Prestige is another reason why certain countries seek WMD. Another factor working against the regimes is the steady diffusion of technology over time—much of the most significant WMD technology is 50 years old, and growing access to dual-use equipment makes it easier for countries or groups to build their own WMD production facilities from commonly available civilian equipment.

There are at least two problems common to all of the nonproliferation regimes—the lack of universal membership and gaps in verification. In the nuclear regime, India, Pakistan, North Korea, and Israel are not members of the NPT. Apart from diplomatic questions about how to treat their status as states with nuclear weapons not sanctioned by the NPT, those countries are not bound by that treaty's prohibition on sharing nuclear technology, nor are they committed to eventually eliminating these weapons. They are also not members of the export control groups. The international community struggles with how to bring these states into the nonproliferation regimes without tacitly agreeing to their acquisition of nuclear weapons. For example, a major objection to the U.S. nuclear cooperation agreement with India was the perception that it legitimizes India's nuclear weapons program without extracting any significant concessions on limiting its nuclear arsenal. Like India, Pakistan is not bound by any NPT obligations, whether or not Pakistani scientist A.Q. Khan sold nuclear technology on the black market with or without Pakistani government acquiescence. Revelations in 2004 of centrifuge enrichment technology sales to Libya, Iran, and North Korea galvanized the international community to examine strengthening implementation of national export controls and interdiction.

In the chemical and biological weapons (CBW) area, some states suspected of having military programs are still outside the treaty. Within the treaties, there are some members (e.g., Iran under the CWC and Russia under the BWC) suspected of continuing programs. In the missile area, although the Hague Code of Conduct has widespread membership, MTCR is still not adhered to by many states (e.g., China, North Korea) that are responsible for proliferating missile technologies.

Continued diplomatic support for the treaties and export control regimes may face some hurdles. In the nuclear nonproliferation regime, many non-weapons states link their continued cooperation with progress in implementing Article VI of the treaty (steps toward eventual nuclear disarmament by the five nuclear weapons states). In recent years, several developments have generated criticism: the United States' abrogation of the Anti-Ballistic Missile (ABM) Treaty; conclusion of the Moscow Treaty, which many criticize as having little real impact and no verification; the U.S. Senate's rejection of the Comprehensive Test Ban Treaty in 1999; failure to proceed on a fissile material production cutoff treaty in Geneva; and perceived interest in new U.S. nuclear weapons. Some non-nuclear-weapon states are also resistant to accepting any limitations on nuclear technology exports involving advanced fuel production technology that has the potential to produce weapons grade material. These states view such restrictions as limiting their access to peaceful nuclear technology as guaranteed by the NPT. Thus, as dual-use equipment in all WMD fields becomes more widespread, there may be a higher expectation that exporters will need to better control where their technology goes and how it is used.

Table 1. Proliferation Control Regimes

Regime	Formal Treaties	Suppliers Groups and Informal Agreements	International Organization	U.S. Legal Framework	U.S. Government Agencies
Nuclear	Nuclear Nonproliferation Treaty (NPT), 1970 Convention on Physical Protection of Nuclear Material, 1987 + Amendment Treaty of Tlatelolco Treaty of Rarotonga Treaty of Pelindaba Treaty of Bangkok Treaty on a nuclear-weapons-free-zone (NWFZ) in Central Asia START Protocols Treaty of Moscow, 2002	Zangger Committee, 1971 Nuclear Suppliers Group, 1975 G-8	International Atomic Energy Agency (IAEA) U.N. Conference on Disarmament	AEA, 1954 NNPA, 1978 FAA, 1961 AECA, 1976 EAA, 1979 NPPA, 1994 Ex-Im Bank, 1945 Nunn-Lugar 1991 Iran-Iraq Arms Non-proliferation (NP) Act, 1992 Iran, Syria, No. Korea NP Act	State, Defense, Commerce, Energy (+ national laboratories), Treasury, NRC, intelligence agencies
Chemical and Biological	Geneva Protocol, 1925 Chemical Weapons Convention (CWC) 1993 Biological and Toxin Weapons Convention (BWC)	Australia Group, 1984	OPCW U.N. Conference on Disarmament	EAA, 1979 AECA, 1976 Biological Weapons Anti-Terrorism Act Chem-Bio Weapons Control Warfare Elimination Act, 1991 Nunn-Lugar Freedom Support Act Iran-Iraq Arms NP Act, 1992 Iran, Syria, No. Korea NP Act	State, Defense, Commerce, Treasury, intelligence agencies
Missiles		Missile Technology Control Regime, 1987 International Code of Conduct, 2002		FAA, 1961 AECA, 1976 EAA, 1979 Missile Tech. Control Act, 1990 Freedom Support Act Iran-Iraq NP Act Iran, Syria, No. Korea NP Act	State, Defense, Commerce, Treasury, NASA intelligence agencies

Source: Congressional Research Service.

Notes: Legislation abbreviations: AEA—Atomic Energy Act; AECA—Arms Export Control Act; EAA—Export Administration Act; FAA—Foreign Assistance Act; NNPA—Nuclear Nonproliferation Act of 1978; NPPA—Nuclear Proliferation Prevention Act.

State-to-State Relations

In addition to a formal framework of control agreements, close political relationships with key allies and other countries are very important for U.S. efforts to counter the spread and the use of WMD. Initiatives by allies, such as the G-8 Global Partnership to Combat the Spread of WMD, demonstrate resolve to tackle specific proliferation problems. In May 2003, President Bush launched the "Proliferation Security Initiative" (see description below). Many of these relationships, nonetheless, are strongly influenced by other political, military, and economic issues that sometimes take precedence over proliferation concerns. In practice, nonproliferation competes with important policy objectives such as trade, regional issues, and domestic political considerations, and uneven implementation of nonproliferation policy can result.

A more difficult challenge exists when U.S. allies and friends seek WMD and missiles of their own or transfer WMD technology. Perhaps the hardest challenge for nonproliferation policies is to reduce the desire of countries for weapons of mass destruction. It is sometimes possible to change regional security conditions through alliances, conventional arms transfers, arms control, or negotiations aimed at settling conflicts. However, eliminating underlying motivations takes time, and the next best option may be to delay WMD development for as long as possible, or to attempt to impact a country's calculation of the costs of pursuing these weapons. Libya's decision in December 2003 to give up its nuclear, chemical weapons, and missile programs is a good example of a state that apparently decided the costs of WMD programs exceeded their benefits.

Unilaterally, the United States uses sanctions to support its nonproliferation objectives. Various laws authorize or require the President to impose unilateral sanctions on countries that acquire, use, or help other countries to obtain WMD or missiles. Sanctions can affect U.S. aid, cooperation, and impose restrictions on U.S. technology exports. The effectiveness of sanctions often depends on persuading other countries to support or respect U.S. sanctions. Even without multilateral support, sanctions can still highlight strong U.S. opposition to WMD proliferation. However, strong sanctions are rarely imposed on U.S. friends or allies that acquire WMD.

Counterproliferation, Intelligence, and Deterrence

U.S. armed forces have developed programs to help prevent the spread of WMD, to deter or prevent their use, and to protect against their effects. Defense cooperation and arms transfers to U.S. allies can ease concerns about security that can lead them to consider acquiring WMD, and also signal potential adversaries that acquisition or use of WMD may evoke a strong military response. U.S. conventional and nuclear military capabilities and the threat of retaliation help deter WMD attacks against U.S. forces, territory, or allies. Counterproliferation capabilities have been expanded in recent years to include more advanced "passive" and "active" defense measures. Passive counterproliferation tools include protective gear such as gas masks and detectors to warn of the presence of WMD. Active measures include missile defenses to protect U.S. territory, forces, and allies; precision-guided penetrating munitions and special operation forces to attack WMD installations; and intelligence gathering and processing capabilities. Intelligence is crucial to U.S. nonproliferation efforts, particularly in helping shape policy options. Intelligence agencies track foreign WMD programs, monitor treaty compliance, and attempt to detect transfers of WMD goods and technology. The United States cooperates with certain allies to prepare for possible counterproliferation actions. Although counterproliferation is a main pillar of U.S. strategy to combat WMD, political and technical hurdles (hidden underground bunkers, locations near civilians, etc.) tend to make counterproliferation a last resort, after other options have failed.

One key tool of counterproliferation has been interdiction of WMD-related equipment shipments at sea, on land, and by air. President Bush announced the Proliferation Security Initiative (PSI) on May 31, 2003. PSI, described as an activity rather than an organization, aims to better coordinate like-minded countries' efforts to interdict such illicit shipments, based on existing legal authorities.[2]

Congressional Role

Congress has been actively engaged in nonproliferation legislation for close to 60 years. In addition to laws affecting diplomacy, treaty implementation and military options, legislation effecting restrictions on foreign aid, sanctions, and export controls helps establish nonproliferation policy and congressional oversight of executive branch nonproliferation and counterproliferation policies.

Congress enacted strict controls on nuclear energy and cooperation in the first Atomic Energy Act of 1946. By the 1950s, however, it became clear that the U.S. nuclear weapons program needed materials from abroad and that pure denial of materials and technology had neither stopped the Soviet Union nor the UK from acquiring nuclear weapons. The 1954 revision of the Atomic Energy Act reflected a shift in strategy from that of prevention through denial to one of influence through cooperation. However, as allies planned to sell sensitive enrichment and reprocessing equipment to states outside of the NPT in the 1970s (e.g., Pakistan, South Korea, and Brazil), Congress reacted by passing several laws to slow down nuclear commerce and implement sanctions against those states clandestinely pursuing nuclear weapons. Controls on exports of chemical and biological agents with military applications and missiles have been regulated under the Arms Export Control Act (AECA) of 1968, and their dual-use technologies have been regulated under the Export Administration Act (EAA) of 1979 and its predecessors, but these controls were implemented relatively later in the 1980s. **Table 2** lists the major U.S. laws enacted to limit the transfer of WMD and WMD technology. Over time, most laws have been amended to address the range of WMD threats, but there are a few laws that address only one kind of weapon of mass destruction; some laws have focused on a proliferation threat from a particular country. Nunn-Lugar-related legislation and the Freedom Support Act address the range of WMD, but focus on Russia and the NIS. In addition, legislation related to Iran and Syria spans the range of WMD proliferation. See **Appendix B** for relevant text from nonproliferation-related legislation.

Organization of the Report

The following sections will describe the nuclear, biological, chemical, and missile nonproliferation regimes. Each section will include (1) a background section with a brief history of the regime; (2) a section setting out the treaties and agreements that authorize or affect the regime; (3) a brief description of how the regime is implemented; (4) U.S. laws authorizing or affecting the regime; and (5) issues for 111th Congress. More detailed information on regime membership, specific provisions in law and relevant executive orders are contained in appendices.

---

[2] See CRS Report RL34327, *Proliferation Security Initiative (PSI)*, by Mary Beth Nikitin.

Table 2. U.S. Legal Framework for Proliferation Control

Title	Public Law	Application	Nuclear	Chemical	Biological	Missiles	Target Country	Notes
Export-Import Bank Act of 1945	P.L. 79-173 P.L. 107-189 reauth	financing cutoff for nuclear safeguards violations and nuclear tests after 1977	X	X	X	X	Various	P.L. 107-189 added enforcement of AECA, EAA, IEEPA as justification for denying financing, extending purview of law to CW/BW/missile areas
Atomic Energy Act 1954	P.L. 83-703	exports; cutoff in nuclear cooperation	X Sec 129				Various	P.L. 95-242 added Sec 129
Foreign Assistance Act 1961	P.L. 87-195	aid cutoff	X Sec 307e Sec 620 E (e) Sec 620 (y)	X	X	X Sec 498 A(b)	Various Russia Cuba	NPPA repealed relevant sections in FAA and placed them in AECA. Reference to FAA is deemed now to refer to sections 101 or 102 in AECA.
Arms Export Control Act 1968	P.L. 90-629	exports, aid cutoff; sanctions	X Sec 3f Sec 101, 102*	X Sec 81 **	X Sec 81	X Sec 72, 73, 74	Various	* NPPA 94 **P.L. 102-182 added in 1991
Nuclear Nonproliferation Act 1978	P.L. 95-242	sanctions	X				Various	See Atomic Energy Act
Export Administration Act 1979	P.L. 96-72	export controls	X Sec 5, 6	X Sec 6(m), 11C	X Sec 6(m), 11C	X Sec 5, 6(l), 11B	Various	Sec 11C added in 1991 by P.L. 102-182.
Biological Anti-Terrorism Act 1989	P.L. 101-298	treaty: BWC			X		N.A.	Implements BWC
Missile Technology Control Act 1990	P.L. 101-510, Title XVII	sanctions				X	Various	Added Chapter VII to AECA, Sections 6 (L) and 11B to EAA 1979
Chemical and Biological Weapons Control and Warfare Elimination Act 1991*	P.L. 102-182, Title III	sanctions		X	X		Various	

Title	Public Law	Application	Nuclear	Chemical	Biological	Missiles	Target Country	Notes
Nunn–Lugar 1991 Cooperative Threat Reduction Act 1993	P.L. 102-228 P.L. 103-160	assistance programs	X	X	X	X	Russia	Amendment to CFE Treaty; Title XI
Iran-Iraq Arms Nonproliferation Act 1992	P.L. 102-484 Title XVI	sanctions	X	X	X	X	Iran, Iraq	
Freedom Support Act	P.L. 102-511 Title V	assistance programs	X	X	X	X	NIS	
Nuclear Proliferation Prevention Act 1994	P.L. 103-236, Title VIII	sanctions	X				Various	Consolidated np legislation into AECA, moving it from FAA
Chemical Weapons Convention Implementation Act 1998	P.L. 105-277	treaty: CWC		X			N.A.	
North Korea Threat Reduction Act of 1999	P.L. 106-113 (consolidated appropriations)	assistance; nuclear cooperation	X				North Korea	
Iran, North Korea and Syria Nonproliferation Act 2006	P.L. 109-112 (amended by P.L. 109-353)	third-party sanctions	X	X	X	X	Iran, North Korea, Syria	Covers transfers to and from states
Syria Accountability and Lebanese Sovereignty Restoration Act of 2003	P.L. 108-175	Export controls, sanctions	X	X	X	X	Syria	
Foreign Operations, Export Financing, and Related Programs Appropriations Act, 2006	P.L. 109-102	Financing, assistance cutoff	X				Russia	
Iran & Libya Sanctions Act	P.L. 109-267 (amended by H.R. 5877)	third-party sanctions	X	X	X	X	Iran, Libya	Renewed by H.R. 6198, Iran Freedom Support Act until 2011, signed by President on Sept. 30, 2006

The Nuclear Nonproliferation Regime

The nuclear nonproliferation regime encompasses several treaties, extensive multilateral and bilateral diplomatic agreements, multilateral organizations and domestic agencies, and the domestic laws of participating countries. Since the dawn of the nuclear age, U.S. leadership has been crucial in developing the regime. While there is almost universal international agreement opposing the further spread of nuclear weapons, several challenges have arisen in recent years: India and Pakistan tested nuclear weapons in 1998; North Korea withdrew from the Nuclear Nonproliferation Treaty (NPT) in 2003 and tested a nuclear device in 2006 and 2009; Libya gave up a clandestine nuclear weapons program in 2004, and Iran was found to be in non-compliance with its treaty obligations in 2005. The discovery of the nuclear black market network run by A.Q. Khan has spurred new thinking about how to strengthen the regime, including enhanced export controls and greater restrictions on sensitive technology. However, the extension of civil nuclear cooperation by the United States and other countries to India, a non-party to the NPT, has raised questions about what benefits still exist for non-nuclear-weapons states that remain within the treaty regime.

In 2009, there were five declared nuclear weapons states (United States, Russia, Great Britain, France, China), three *de facto* nuclear weapons states (India, Israel, Pakistan), and one country— North Korea—that has probably produced enough plutonium for at least half a dozen nuclear bombs and has tested two nuclear devices.[3] This is considerably less than predicted 40 years ago, when President Kennedy warned of the possibility that, by the 1970s, the United States could "face a world in which fifteen or twenty or twenty-five nations may have these weapons."

The nonproliferation regime has not stopped all proliferation, but it has helped restrain nuclear ambitions and solidified an international norm of behavior strongly condemning proliferation. Many countries that could make nuclear weapons have not, but some have at one time or another taken significant steps towards acquiring a nuclear weapons capability. Argentina, Brazil, South Africa, Iran, Iraq, North Korea, Taiwan, Sweden, and South Korea all have had nuclear weapons development programs. Both Japan and Germany had nuclear weapons programs during the Second World War, but did not succeed in making nuclear weapons before their programs were halted at the end of the war. Argentina, Brazil, South Korea, Sweden, Taiwan, and South Africa abandoned their nuclear weapons programs and joined the NPT as non-nuclear-weapons states. South Africa was the only country in this group to have built and abandoned actual warheads.[4] Ukraine, Kazakhstan, and Belarus inherited nuclear weapons on their soil when the Soviet Union collapsed, but opted to join the NPT as non-nuclear-weapons states (the warheads were returned to Russia). Despite its membership as a non-nuclear-weapons state in the NPT, Libya gave up a clandestine nuclear weapons program in December 2003.[5]

While only a few countries maintain an interest in developing nuclear weapons, it is difficult to predict how many countries or terrorist groups may in the future want a nuclear weapons

---

[3] For a current summary, see CRS Report RL30699, *Nuclear, Biological, and Chemical Weapons and Missiles: Status and Trends*, by Paul K. Kerr.

[4] For details, see "South Africa Profile: Nuclear Overview," Nuclear Threat Initiative website, http://www nti.org/ e_research/profiles/SAfrica/Nuclear/index_2153 html.

[5] See CRS Report RS21823, *Disarming Libya: Weapons of Mass Destruction*, by Sharon Squassoni.

capability. Some of the major challenges in preventing nuclear proliferation will include the following:

- controlling access to sensitive nuclear fuel cycle technologies, such as uranium enrichment and spent fuel reprocessing, via multilateral ownership or some other mechanism;

- strengthening physical protection of all source and special nuclear materials globally, with continued emphasis on controlling nuclear materials smuggling from the former Soviet Union and other countries with weak controls;

- strengthening the International Atomic Energy Agency's safeguards system;

- strengthening national export control laws and regulations, per U.N. Security Council Resolution 1540;

- negotiating with North Korea to verify and dismantle its nuclear weapons program;

- restraining nuclear proliferation in India and Pakistan;

- restraining nuclear programs in the Middle East, including those of Israel and Iran;

- preventing U.S. technology from aiding the development of WMD and delivery systems in foreign countries;

- strengthening international verification and enforcement of nonproliferation agreements.

Treaties and Agreements

The NPT is the centerpiece of nuclear nonproliferation efforts. Other relevant treaties include regional nuclear-weapon-free zones and the Convention on the Physical Protection of Nuclear Material. In addition to these multilateral treaties, the United States has also entered into bilateral agreements and multilateral initiatives, such as the G-8 Global Partnership to Combat WMD. Finally, actions the United States takes in related areas of arms control may have an impact on the nonproliferation regime.

Treaty on the Nonproliferation of Nuclear Weapons (NPT), 1970

It took just three months after the bombing of Hiroshima and Nagasaki in 1945 for the first proposals to emerge from governments to control the "destructive uses" of nuclear energy. It took 25 years, however, for the NPT to emerge as the blueprint for nuclear nonproliferation.[6] In 1968, the treaty demarcated nuclear-weapon states from non-nuclear-weapon states by defining nuclear-weapon states as those states that have manufactured and exploded a nuclear weapon or other

---

[6] Previous proposals included a 1945 proposal by the United States, Britain, and Canada proposed to establish a U.N. Atomic Energy Commission to eliminate "the use of atomic energy for destructive purposes," a 1957 "package" of measures (from Canada, UK, France, and United States) to the U.N. Disarmament Commission that included a commitment not to transfer nuclear weapons, a 1964 program proposed by the United States for nonproliferation. See *Arms Control and Disarmament Agreements: Texts and Histories of the Negotiations*, 1990 edition, U.S. Arms Control and Disarmament Agency, p. 89.

nuclear explosive device prior to January 1, 1967. This definition implied that there would only ever be five "legitimate" nuclear-weapon states—the United States, Russia, Great Britain, France, and China. All other states would join as non-nuclear-weapon states, agreeing not to acquire nuclear weapons in exchange for assistance in the peaceful uses of nuclear energy. As of January 2010, there are 189 parties to the NPT, including all five nuclear weapons states.[7] Only four countries are not members of the treaty. North Korea withdrew from the treaty officially in April 2003. India, Israel, and Pakistan have never been members of the treaty.

The pledge not to acquire nuclear weapons is verified through the application of "nuclear safeguards" measures. The International Atomic Energy Agency (IAEA), founded in 1957, devised a system of nuclear material accountancy coupled with periodic and special inspections to ensure that nuclear material is not diverted from peaceful uses to military uses. Each non-nuclear-weapon-state party to the NPT must negotiate an agreement with the IAEA to submit all nuclear material in its possession to regular inspections.[8] After learning several lessons from Iraq's and North Korea's clandestine nuclear programs, the IAEA launched a major effort to strengthen its safeguards system (see below) in 1992.

The incentive for non-nuclear-weapon states to submit to inspections is a promise by advanced nuclear countries to promote "the fullest possible exchange of equipment, materials and scientific and technological information for the peaceful uses of nuclear energy."[9] For their part, the nuclear-weapon states agree to "pursue negotiations in good faith on effective measures relating to cessation of the nuclear arms race at an early date and to nuclear disarmament."[10]

In 1995, NPT members voted to make the treaty permanent. The members also agreed on a stronger review process to oversee compliance with the treaty. However, many members of the NPT are dissatisfied, particularly with perceived lack of progress on nuclear disarmament, and the future of the treaty is not guaranteed (see discussion of implementation). Member states will discuss the status of the treaty at a Review Conference in May 2010.

Convention on the Physical Protection of Nuclear Material, 1987

The Convention on the Physical Protection of Nuclear Material[11] sets international standards for nuclear trade and commerce. The treaty had 142 parties in January 2010. The convention outlines security requirements for the protection of nuclear materials against terrorism and provides for the prosecution and punishment of offenders of international nuclear trade laws. Parties to the treaty agree to report to the IAEA on the disposition of nuclear materials being transported and agree to provide appropriate security during such transport.

---

[7] This number excludes North Korea (the DPRK). North Korea announced its withdrawal from the NPT effective January 11, 2003, but no official agreement has been reached on its status amongst the NPT states parties or depositary states.

[8] These agreements are called "full-scope safeguards." Other states have partial safeguards agreements, including India, Pakistan and Israel, which can either apply to material or facilities. All of the five nuclear weapons states have voluntary safeguards agreements, which cover a portion of facilities and materials.

[9] NPT, Article IV-2.

[10] NPT, Article VI.

[11] http://www.iaea.org/Publications/Documents/Conventions/cppnm.html.

For several years, the United States worked to strengthen this treaty to address nuclear terrorism by extending controls to domestic facility security, not just transportation. In July 2005, states parties convened to amend the convention. They extended the convention's scope to cover not only nuclear material in international transport, but also nuclear material in domestic use, storage, and transport, as well as the protection of nuclear material and facilities from sabotage. The new rules will come into effect once they have been ratified by two-thirds of the states parties of the convention, which could take several years. As of December 17, 2009, only 33 states had deposited their instruments of ratification, acceptance, or approval of the amendment with the depositary. On September 4, 2007, President Bush submitted the amendment to the Senate for its advice and consent on ratification. The Senate Committee on Foreign Relations recommended that the Senate give its advice and consent on September 11, 2008. The Senate must approve implementing legislation before the United States deposits its instrument of ratification to the amendment.

Related Arms Control Agreements

In the 1990s, the Comprehensive Test Ban Treaty (CTBT) was seen as the next step toward nuclear disarmament, but also a means to prevent the further spread of nuclear weapons. By the mid-1990s, all nuclear-weapons states were observing a moratorium on testing, which the treaty would make permanent. The parties completed negotiations and signed the CTBT in 1996; President Clinton submitted the treaty to the Senate in September 1997, and in 1999 the Senate voted against the treaty.[12] President Obama has said his Administration will pursue U.S. CTBT ratification.

Another initiative dating from the 1990s is the effort to negotiate a treaty banning the production of fissile materials for weapons, or fissile material cut-off treaty (FMCT). Some perceive such a ban on producing fissile material for weapons as much more relevant today than it was a decade ago. Concern about terrorist access to large stockpiles of fissile material has only grown since the Cooperative Threat Reduction programs began in the early 1990s and particularly since September 11, 2001. Revelations about Pakistani scientist A.Q. Khan's nuclear black market sales of uranium enrichment technology in 2004 have spurred efforts not only to shut down networks, but restrict even "legitimate" technology transfer. Recent proposals to strengthen the nonproliferation regime, including those of Mohamed El Baradei, former director general of the International Atomic Energy Agency (IAEA), have focused on tighter controls on sensitive nuclear fuel cycle technologies, renewed disarmament effort, and creative approaches toward states outside the Nuclear Nonproliferation Treaty (NPT)—India, Pakistan, and Israel.[13] An FMCT could play a pivotal role in implementing that agenda, by helping to gain broad support for new multilateral arrangements to restrict enrichment and reprocessing, helping to strengthen consensus among NPT parties, and by achieving a concrete step toward disarmament.[14] The Obama Administration said it will "lead a global effort to negotiate a verifiable treaty ending the production of fissile materials for weapons purposes."[15]

---

[12] See CRS Report RL33548, *Comprehensive Nuclear-Test-Ban Treaty: Background and Current Developments*, by Jonathan Medalia.

[13] Mohamed ElBaradei, "Rethinking Nuclear Safeguards," *Washington Post,* June 14, 2006.

[14] Henry Kissinger, Sam Nunn, William Perry and George Shultz, "A World Free of Nuclear Weapons," *Wall Street Journal*, January 4, 2007. http://www.nuclearsecurityproject.org/site/c.mjJXJbMMIoE/b.3483737/k.4057/Nuclear_Security_Project_Home.htm

[15] http://www.whitehouse.gov/agenda/homeland_security/.

Nuclear-Weapon-Free Zones

In the last 35 years, some states have concluded treaties to declare their regions to be "nuclear weapons-free." These regions now include most of the globe—Latin America, Central and Southeast Asia, the South Pacific, Africa, and Central Asia.

Treaty for the Prohibition of Nuclear Weapons in Latin America (Treaty of Tlatelolco)

The Treaty of Tlatelolco[16] establishes a nuclear-weapon-free zone (NWFZ) in Latin America. Protocol I of the treaty obligates non-Latin American countries that have territories in the zone (United States, UK, Netherlands, France) to accept the provisions of the treaty with respect to those territories. Protocol II contains a negative security pledge by the nuclear weapons states (China, France, Russia, UK, United States) "not to use or threaten to use nuclear weapons against the Contracting Parties of the Treaty." In 1994, treaty holdouts Argentina, Brazil, and Chile signed on, and in 1995 Cuba signed the treaty (which entered into force in 2002). The Agency for the Prohibition of Nuclear Weapons in Latin America and the Caribbean (OPANAL) in Mexico City serves as Secretariat for treaty implementation.

South Pacific Nuclear Free Zone (Treaty of Rarotonga)

Thirteen nations of the South Pacific have established a NWFZ for their region which prohibits the possession of nuclear weapons by its members and bans the manufacture or permanent emplacement of nuclear weapons within the zone by signatories outside of the Pacific region. The treaty does not inhibit transit through the zone by nuclear-armed or -powered military ships or aircraft. In 1996, the United States, France, and Britain signed the protocols to the treaty, which are nearly identical to those of the Treaty of Tlatelolco. Before signing the treaty protocols, France conducted its last nuclear tests at its test site in French Polynesia. The United States is the only nuclear-weapon state that has not ratified the protocol.

African Nuclear Weapon-Free-Zone Treaty (Treaty of Pelindaba)

In April 1996, the Treaty of Pelindaba, establishing Africa as a NWFZ, was opened for signature. The treaty now has 53 signatures and 21 ratifications. It will enter into force after the 28th ratification. The African NWFZ closely follows the models of the South Pacific and Latin American zones, and thus was able to attract the support of the United States and other weapons states after certain criteria were satisfied. This nuclear-weapon-free zone is not yet in force, and the United States and Russia have not ratified (but have signed) the relevant protocol.

Southeast Asia Nuclear Weapon-Free-Zone (Treaty of Bangkok)

A group of 10 Southeast Asian nations declared a NWFZ for their region in December 1995, and the treaty entered into force in 1997. The United States and other weapons states declined to sign the protocols to the zone because the treaty contained controversial definitions of its members' sovereignty over territorial seas. The United States maintains that the language of the treaty is

---

[16] See http://www.opanal.org/index-i.html.

inconsistent with the Law of the Sea and could inflame territorial disputes as well as interfere with rights of passage. Modifications of the language are under consideration. In 1999, China announced it would sign the protocol but has deferred its signature.

Central Asian Nuclear Weapons Free Zone

Signed on September 8, 2006, this treaty creates a NWFZ in the five Central Asian states of Kazakhstan, Kyrgyzstan, Tajikistan, Turkmenistan, and Uzbekistan. With Kazakhstan's ratification in January 2009, all five countries have joined the treaty. The treaty entered into force on March 21, 2009. This treaty is the first nuclear weapon-free zone located entirely in the northern hemisphere, and prohibits the development, manufacture, stockpiling, acquisition, or possession of any nuclear explosive device within the zone. The treaty requires signatories to accept enhanced IAEA safeguards on nuclear material and activities, addresses the impact of production and testing of Soviet nuclear weapons on the environment, and implements measures to meet international standards for nuclear facility security.

Other Agreements

The United States has concluded arrangements with several states on a bilateral basis and on a multilateral basis in an effort to address specific proliferation challenges. In 1994, the United States signed the Agreed Framework with North Korea (which was terminated in 2003) and now addresses the North Korean nuclear program through the Six Party Talks. The United States addresses the Iranian nuclear program with the other permanent members of the U.N. Security Council plus Germany in the "P-5+1" Contact Group. The United States also provides bilateral assistance to countries to secure their WMD-relevant materials and technologies, or to detect their movement across borders.

In 2002, the United States initiated a "10 plus 10 over 10" effort within the G-8 to provide additional funding for nonproliferation assistance to Russia and the newly independent states of the former Soviet Union (NIS), called the G-8 Global Partnership Against the Spread of Weapons and Materials of Mass Destruction. The United States also created the Proliferation Security Initiative in 2003 to improve coordination on WMD interdiction efforts. The U.S.-Russian-led Global Initiative to Combat Nuclear Terrorism also aims to guide and coordinate international activities. The establishment of these joint activities reflected a trend away from internationally negotiated approaches to proliferation controls and towards ad hoc cooperation amongst "like-minded states," at least during the Bush Administration's tenure, and due to heightened perception of WMD threats following the attacks of September 11, 2001.

G-8 Global Partnership

At a summit held in June 2002 in Kananaskis, Canada, G-8 members agreed to a Global Partnership to halt the spread of weapons of mass destruction and related materials and technology. The G-8 members agreed to raise $20 billion over 10 years in nonproliferation—related assistance beginning Russia, of which the United States committed to providing $10B. Projects relating to disarmament, nonproliferation, counterterrorism and nuclear safety initially were to focus on Russia. Russia and, since 2004, Ukraine are the official recipients of Global Partnership funds. Since 2002, 12 countries and the European Union have joined the G-8 as donors. The four priority areas of work as identified at the Kananaskis Summit are (1) destruction of chemical weapons, (2) dismantlement of decommissioned nuclear submarines, (3) disposition of fissile materials, and (4) employment of former weapons scientists. Some donor countries also emphasize the importance of biological weapons-related and nuclear material security assistance. A G8 Global Partnership Working Group meets regularly to coordinate assistance efforts, and publishes a report and annex detailing projects at the summit each year.[17]

At the June 2004 Sea Island summit, the Global Partnership states agreed to consider expanding assistance to states outside the former Soviet Union. At their 2008 and 2009 summits, the G-8 countries agreed to extend the Global Partnership to recipients worldwide on a case-by-case basis. This would mirror U.S. efforts to expand its own cooperative threat reduction assistance to states outside of Russia and the former Soviet Union, for example, Albania. Outside observers assess that pledges are about $2 billion short of the $20 billion goal, and there remains a gap between pledges and actual funds spent. The Global Partnership is expected to be a main focus of the G8 Summit in 2010, as the initiative nears its 10-year anniversary and since Canada holds the G-8 presidency. Global Partnership countries will be examining whether and how to extend the initiative beyond its first 10 years. The U.S. government supports the further expansion of Global Partnership recipients and an extension of the effort beyond 2012.

Global Initiative to Combat Nuclear Terrorism

At the July 2006 summit, the United States and Russia launched another initiative—the Global Initiative to Combat Nuclear Terrorism. As of July 2008, 76 states have agreed to the statement of principles and are Global Initiative partner nations. The International Atomic Energy Agency (IAEA), the European Union (EU) and International Criminal Police Organization (INTERPOL) have observer status. Although it does not receive funding of its own, the initiative appears to exceed the G-8 Global Partnership in its scope. Participating states share a common goal to improve national capabilities to combat nuclear terrorism by sharing best practices through multinational exercises and expert level meetings. Without dues or a secretariat, actions under the Initiative will take legal guidance from the International Convention on the Suppression of Acts of Nuclear Terrorism, the Convention on the Physical Protection of Nuclear Materials and its amendment, and U.N. Security Council Resolutions 1540 and 1373.[18] According to a White House fact sheet issued at the time of its announcement, the initiative has the following goals:[19]

- Improve security of nuclear material and radioactive substances and nuclear facilities;

- Detect and prevent illicit trafficking in such materials, especially by terrorists;

- Develop responses to nuclear terrorist attacks;

- Cooperate in developing technical means to combat nuclear terrorism;

---

[17] For the 2009 G8 Summit documentation see the Italian Presidency's website: http://www.g8italia2009.it/G8/Home/ G8-G8_Layout_locale-1199882116809_Atti htm

[18] "U.S.-Russia Joint Fact Sheet on The Global Initiative to Combat Nuclear Terrorism," July 15, 2006. Available at http://www.state.gov/r/pa/prs/ps/2006/69016 htm.

[19] http://www.whitehouse.gov/news/releases/2006/07/20060715-3 html.

- Take all possible measures to deny safe haven to terrorists seeking to acquire or use nuclear materials; and

- Strengthen national legal frameworks to ensure the effective prosecution of terrorists.

Global Initiative partner nations met in June 2009 in the Hague to discuss "enhancing international partnerships by sharing best practices." In past meetings the partner countries have focused on strengthening detection and forensics; denying safe haven and financing to terrorists; deterring terrorist intentions to acquire and use nuclear devices. Participants have developed "Model Nuclear Detection Guidelines." An International Nuclear Terrorism Law Enforcement Conference, organized by the FBI, was held in Miami in June 2007 for Global Initiative partners. Tabletop and field exercises are held to identify and address individual states' vulnerabilities. According to a State Department fact sheet, over 30 workshops and exercises have been held since the initiative began.[20] President Obama proposed in an April 2009 speech in Prague that the Global Initiative should become a "durable, international institution" but it is not yet clear how this will be carried out.

Proliferation Security Initiative[21]

President Bush announced the Proliferation Security Initiative (PSI) in May 2003 to improve multilateral cooperation in interdicting shipments of weapons of mass destruction-related materials and delivery systems at sea, on land, and in the air. U.S. officials stress that PSI is a voluntary effort consistent with national legal authorities and international law. The stated purpose is to strengthen the enforcement of already-existing export controls associated with nonproliferation treaties, and to better coordinate interdiction efforts through multilateral training exercises. States agreed to a set of interdiction principles in Paris in September 2003 and 90 nations now support PSI. PSI participants conduct joint interdiction training exercises and hold regular operational experts working group meetings. The United States is pursuing the conclusion of ship-boarding agreements with key states that have high volumes of international shipping. The United States has signed such agreements with the Bahamas, Belize, Croatia, Cyprus, Liberia, Malta, the Marshall Islands, Mongolia, and Panama. The Obama Administration has given full support to PSI and has said it wants to strengthen and "institutionalize" the effort.[22]

U.N. Security Council Resolution 1540

In April 2004, the U.N. Security Council adopted Resolution 1540, which requires all states to "criminalize proliferation, enact strict export controls and secure all sensitive materials within their borders." UNSCR 1540 called on states to enforce effective domestic controls over WMD and WMD-related materials in production, use, storage, and transport; to maintain effective border controls; and to develop national export and trans-shipment controls over such items, all of which should help interdiction efforts. The resolution did not, however, provide any enforcement authority, nor did it specifically mention interdiction. About two-thirds of all states have reported to the U.N. on their efforts to strengthen defenses against WMD trafficking. U.N. Security Council Resolutions 1673 (2006) and 1810 (2008) extended the duration of the 1540 Committee.

---

[20] http://www.state.gov/t/isn/rls/fs/125325 htm

[21] For a detailed discussion, see CRS Report RL34327, *Proliferation Security Initiative (PSI)*, by Mary Beth Nikitin.

[22] "The Agenda: Homeland Security," White House website, http://www.whitehouse.gov/agenda/homeland_security/

The committee is currently focused on identifying assistance projects for states in need and matching donors to improve these WMD controls.

Implementing the Regime

Although the Nuclear Nonproliferation Treaty (NPT) is perhaps the most visible aspect of the nuclear nonproliferation regime, the success of nonproliferation efforts relies on the sturdy functioning of national export control laws and their implementation, the Zangger Committee and Nuclear Suppliers Group multilateral coordination of export controls, and effective inspections conducted by the International Atomic Energy Agency (IAEA). Equally important is the *quid pro quo* of technical assistance in the peaceful uses of nuclear energy that the IAEA provides.

The International Atomic Energy Agency (IAEA)

The IAEA, a U.N.-affiliated international organization, was established in 1957 to "accelerate and enlarge the contribution of atomic energy to peace, health and prosperity," and to ensure "that assistance provided by it ... is not used in such a way as to further any military purpose."[23] With the entry into force of the NPT in 1970, it performs the dual missions of verifying NPT obligations and providing assistance in peaceful nuclear technology to developing nations. By December 2009, the agency had 151 member states and an annual budget of about $400 million.[24] The IAEA safeguards system monitors nuclear materials and technology to deter and detect diversions from peaceful to military uses.

The administrative structure of the agency resembles that of the United Nations. The General Conference includes all members and meets annually. The Board of Governors has 35 members, nine of which are permanent advanced nuclear nations, with the remaining board members serving one-year terms as representatives of regional nuclear interests. The Secretariat is the administrative arm of the agency. It is headed by the director general, who is the chief policy-making official. The current director general, Yukiya Amano, is a Japanese diplomat. The IAEA won the Nobel Peace Prize in 2005 under its previous director general, Mohamed El Baradei.

In over 25 years of inspections, five states have been declared in violation of their safeguards agreements: Iraq, North Korea, Romania, Libya, and Iran. Following revelations in 1991 of Iraq's clandestine activities, the IAEA developed a strengthened safeguards program (formerly called "93+2") to improve its ability to detect unreported nuclear activities in non-weapons states. The program includes

- provision of intelligence information to the IAEA by member states about suspect nuclear activities;
- access for inspectors to any location on a timely basis;
- new safeguards technology;
- measures to promote complete transparency and reporting of all nuclear commerce;

---

[23] The IAEA Statute is found at http://www.iaea.org/About/statute html.

[24] See http://www.iaea.org/About/index html.

- sufficient financial resources to carry out the IAEA's expanded responsibilities.

State parties to the NPT have been required to ratify new "model protocol" agreements to their existing nuclear safeguards agreements with the IAEA (INFCIRC/540). President Bush submitted the U.S. model protocol agreement to the Senate for its consent to ratification in 2002. The Senate gave its advice and consent to the protocol on March 31, 2004 (Treaty Doc. 107-7, Senate Executive Report 108-12). On December 18, 2006, implementing legislation was passed in P.L. 109-401, as part of the Hyde Act. On December 30, 2008, the President signed the instrument of ratification for the Additional Protocol. It was deposited with the IAEA and entered into force on January 6, 2009. A continuing issue will be adequate funding for the IAEA safeguards. The annual safeguards budget is insufficient to carry out the IAEA's new responsibilities; the agency relies on extrabudgetary (voluntary) contributions to fully fund its work. Thus, the IAEA's ability to carry out its growing responsibilities and efforts to upgrade its safeguards system continue to be limited by members' reluctance to increase the IAEA regular budget. The United States had advocated for increasing the budget of the IAEA.

Since September 11, 2001, the IAEA has been promoting efforts to help prevent terrorists from acquiring or using weapons of mass destruction, including nuclear or radiological devices. These have focused primarily on upgrading its assistance in physical security, in locating orphaned radioactive sources, and in promoting enhancement of the Convention on the Protection of Physical Security. The IAEA established a Code of Conduct on the Safety and Security of Radioactive Sources in 2001 and an Action Plan on Combating Nuclear Terrorism in 2002. In 2005, the IAEA Board of Governors adopted a four-year Nuclear Security Plan 2006-2009.[25] In 2009, a Nuclear Security Action Plan for 2010-2013 was outlined. The Nuclear Security Fund (NSF) is a voluntary funding mechanism to support activities to prevent, detect, and respond to nuclear terrorism. Implementation of the Nuclear Security Plan is dependent on contributions to the NSF.[26] As of September 2009, 107 states participate in the IAEA's Illicit Trafficking Database, which facilitates the exchange of information related to the illicit trafficking of nuclear or radiological material.

In response to revelations in 2004 about Pakistani scientist A.Q. Khan's clandestine nuclear sales to Libya, Iran, and North Korea, the IAEA's director general proposed seven steps to enhance the nuclear nonproliferation regime. These include a five-year moratorium on construction of uranium enrichment and plutonium reprocessing facilities; conversion of nuclear reactors using highly enriched uranium (HEU) to low-enriched uranium; making the Additional Protocol the verification norm of the NPT; revisiting U.N. Security Council actions in response to a state's withdrawal from the NPT; universal implementation of U.N. Security Council Resolution 1540; acceleration of Article VI actions by nuclear weapons states (toward nuclear disarmament); and resolution of regional security tensions that give rise to proliferation, including a Middle East nuclear-weapon-free zone.[27] Measures to further strengthen the non-proliferation aspects of the IAEA's work meet resistant by member states who are more concerned about access to peaceful use of nuclear technology. In particular, the case of Iran's noncompliance with its safeguards obligations continues to present challenges for the IAEA and the nonproliferation regime.

---

[25] See GC(50)/RES/11.

[26] See GOV/2007/43-GC(51)/15.

[27] IAEA Director General Mohamed ElBaradei, "Seven Steps to Raise World Security," *Financial Times*, February 2, 2005.

The Nuclear Suppliers Group (NSG)

In 1971, a group of seven NPT nuclear supplier nations formed the Nuclear Exporters Committee, known as the Zangger Committee, to assist in restricting nuclear trade as called for in Article III of the NPT.[28] In 1974, the Zangger Committee compiled a list of nuclear export items that could be potentially useful for military applications of nuclear technology. The nuclear suppliers agreed that the transfer of items on the list would "trigger" a requirement for IAEA safeguards to ensure that the items were not used to make nuclear explosives. The Zangger list included reactors, reactor components, and certain nuclear materials such as heavy water. In recent years, the list of controlled items has been expanded and updated. Membership is voluntary and implies no formal commitments for enforcement of the guidelines. As of January 2010, the Zangger Committee had 37 members,[29] including all five NPT-recognized nuclear weapon states. The committee meets twice each year to exchange information and upgrade its list of controlled commodities.

Shaken by the 1974 test of a nuclear explosive device by India, the major nuclear suppliers in 1975 established a set of unpublished nuclear export guidelines.[30] In 1978, the group, known as the London Club, added new members and announced a common policy regarding nuclear exports. While the NPT's Zangger list initially included only nuclear materials and components used directly in weapons development, the London Club adopted more restrictive export control guidelines that included some dual-use items, with civil and military applications. The NSG guidelines called for suppliers to exercise restraint regarding transfers of enrichment and reprocessing technology, and required the provision of physical security for transferred nuclear facilities and materials, acceptance of safeguards on replicated facilities (based on a design transferred from a London Club member-state), and prohibitions against retransfer of nuclear exports to third parties.

Although NSG guidelines were in place, members took no further actions until 1991. Concerned about Iraq's successful procurement of dual-use items and apparently inconsistent enforcement of nuclear export controls in several supplier countries, the NSG convened in March 1991 for the first time since 1978 to update its list of controlled commodities. The expanded group agreed on new guidelines in January 1992 for transfers of a wider range of nuclear-related, dual-use equipment, material and technology and jointly adopted the long-standing U.S. policy of requiring full-scope safeguards for all nuclear exports. (Nations purchasing nuclear technology must open *all* nuclear facilities to inspection, not just the facility in which an imported item is used.)[31] The NSG has expanded to 45 members.[32]

Some developing nations have objected to the NSG because it further divides the technologically advanced nuclear "haves" from the "have nots" and creates additional obstacles to their access to nuclear technology. A few countries have turned to suppliers outside of the NSG to avoid the requirement for full-scope safeguards on nuclear exports. The emergence of new nuclear

---

[28] See http://www.zanggercommittee.org/Zangger/default.htm for Zangger website.

[29] See **Appendix A** for list of Zangger Committee members. http://www.zanggercommittee.org/Zangger/default htm.

[30] See http://www.nuclearsuppliersgroup.org for NSG website.

[31] The new guidelines appeared as an International Atomic Energy Agency document, INFCIRC/254/Rev.1/Part 1 and Part 2, July 1992.

[32] See **Appendix A** for NSG membership.

suppliers that do not subscribe to NSG guidelines undermines the efforts of NSG members to control the spread of nuclear weapons.

The strengthening of NSG export policy after the Gulf War responded to numerous examples of illegal, covert, and suspicious nuclear trade involving Western firms and countries such as India, Iraq, Iran, Israel, Pakistan, Brazil, Argentina, South Africa, and others. These transfers underscored the limitations of voluntary export controls, but they also motivated U.S. officials to push for further tightening of NSG restrictions on world nuclear exports. However, as a voluntary association, the NSG has no formal administrative structure, no legal authority to influence the nuclear trade policies of its members, and no formal enforcement mechanism.

In 2005, the United States approached the NSG to create an exception for India to the NSG's requirement for full-scope safeguards as a condition of nuclear supply. Such an exception was necessary for the United States to implement its proposed civil nuclear cooperation initiative with India.[33] Key NSG members, such as the United States, Russia, and France, supported a country-specific exception, while other members questioned whether such an approach might be damaging to the nonproliferation regime. India and the IAEA formulated an India-specific safeguards agreement, as required by the Henry J. Hyde United States-India Peaceful Atomic Energy Cooperation Act of 2006 (P.L. 109-401) in 2008. In September 2008, the NSG agreed to exempt India from the full-scope safeguards requirement, although retained a policy of restraint on the transfer enrichment and reprocessing equipment. NSG members are discussing whether or not to adopt additional guidelines that would define eligibility criteria for the transfer of enrichment and reprocessing technologies to new states.

U.S. Government Organization

The Departments of State, Energy, Defense, Treasury, and Commerce, and the intelligence community are all involved in the formulation and implementation of nonproliferation policy.[34] Congress mandated the creation of a White House Coordinator for the Prevention of Weapons of Mass Destruction Proliferation and Terrorism (P.L. 110-53). The Administration pledged to appoint "a deputy national security advisor to be in charge of coordinating all U.S. programs aimed at reducing the risk of nuclear terrorism and weapons proliferation."[35] Gary Samore was assigned this post, as National Security Council Coordinator for Arms Control and Nonproliferation. Primary functions of the various federal agencies are outlined below.

- The National Security Council coordinates nonproliferation, counterproliferation, threat reduction, and WMD terrorism prevention policy.

- The State Department, in consultation with the Energy Department, negotiates U.S. agreements for nuclear cooperation and arms control measures, represents U.S. nonproliferation interests with other states and international organizations such as the IAEA, and administers some nonproliferation assistance programs. The State Department also represents the United States and plans international

---

[33] See CRS Report RL33016, *U.S. Nuclear Cooperation with India: Issues for Congress*, by Paul K. Kerr.

[34] An October 2007 GAO Report raises important questions about US efforts to combat proliferation networks. See U.S. General Accounting Office, "U.S. Efforts to Combat Nuclear Networks Need Better Data on Proliferation Risks and Program Results," October 31, 2007. http://www.gao.gov/new.items/d0821.pdf.

[35] http://www.whitehouse.gov/agenda/homeland_security/

coordination meetings for the G8 Global Partnership, Global Initiative to Combat Nuclear Terrorism, and Proliferation Security Initiative.

- The Department of Defense is responsible for counterproliferation strategy and policy, administers the Cooperative Threat Reduction (CTR) programs, and is involved in operational aspects of the Proliferation Security Initiative.

- The Department of Energy's National Nuclear Security Administration provides technical expertise in nuclear weapons to support nonproliferation policy and diplomacy, largely through its national laboratories. DOE also administers nonproliferation programs to control fissile material in the former Soviet Union and elsewhere, the Global Threat Reduction Initiative and export control and border security programs.

- The Nuclear Regulatory Commission licenses nuclear exports subject to concurrence by the Department of State.

- The Department of Commerce oversees licensing of dual-use exports as mandated by Section 309(c) of the Nuclear Non-proliferation Act, which requires controls on "all export items, other than those licensed by the NRC, which could be, if used for purposes other than those for which the export is intended, of significance for nuclear explosive purposes."

- The Department of the Treasury oversees U.S. embargoes through its Office of Foreign Assets Control, and enforces export control through the U.S. Customs Service. It also represents the United States in the inter-governmental Financial Action Task Force (FATF).

- The Director of National Intelligence has a National Counterproliferation Center (NCPC) that coordinates intelligence on proliferation issues within the intelligence community.

- The Federal Bureau of Investigation (FBI) has a WMD Directorate.

- Several interagency working groups coordinate the various responsibilities for nonproliferation policy.

Since September 11, 2001, significant U.S. government interest has focused on counterproliferation programs—that is, military measures against weapons of mass destruction. Although the Department of Defense has had programs in place for several years, efforts in this area have been renewed. Counterproliferation includes active and passive defenses to protect U.S. and allied troops. The December 2002 National Strategy to Combat Weapons of Mass Destruction described counterproliferation as including interdiction, deterrence, defense, and mitigation.[36] Preemption is explicitly described as an option under defense and mitigation policies. Increased attention has also been given to breaking down proliferation finance networks. U.S. government agencies have also stepped up efforts to secure or remove nuclear and radiological materials worldwide and to improve detection of WMD-related trafficking at borders. President Obama has pledged to secure all vulnerable nuclear materials around the world in four years. A Global Nuclear Security Summit will be held in April 2010 to further this goal.

---

[36] "National Strategy to Combat Weapons of Mass Destruction," December 11, 2002. See http://www.whitehouse.gov/news/releases/2002/12/WMDStrategy.pdf.

U.S. Laws[37]

The main legislative pillars of U.S. nuclear nonproliferation policy are the Atomic Energy Act of 1954, as amended by the Nuclear Nonproliferation Act of 1978, and the Arms Export Control Act of 1968.

The Atomic Energy Act of 1954 (AEA)[38]

The Atomic Energy Act of 1954 established legal authority for the commercial and military development of nuclear energy. It gave primary authority for the development and oversight of the U.S. government's nuclear programs to a civilian agency: the Atomic Energy Commission (now the Nuclear Regulatory Commission). In 1974, these duties were divided between the NRC and the Department of Energy. A major purpose of the act was to establish controls on the export of nuclear materials, goods, information, and technology. Under the AEA, the State Department must negotiate an agreement for nuclear cooperation as a precondition for exports of sensitive U.S. nuclear technology to any foreign country. Each agreement must meet several standards outlined in the AEA. Moreover, the act contains penalties and restrictions for countries that do not uphold the terms of nuclear agreements with the United States. Congress reviews all such agreements before they can enter into force.

The Nuclear Non-Proliferation Act of 1978 (NNPA)[39]

Congress and the Carter Administration viewed U.S. leadership and control over the international nuclear fuel cycle as an effective means of restraining the spread of uranium enrichment and plutonium reprocessing facilities throughout the world. Enrichment and reprocessing technologies are key technologies for states aspiring to develop nuclear weapons. While reaffirming the U.S. commitment to be a reliable supplier of nuclear technology and fuels, the act established an important new requirement for nations importing U.S. nuclear technology and materials: they must accept full-scope safeguards on their entire nuclear program. This standard was adopted by NSG members in 1992. The act also established a requirement of prior U.S. approval for retransfers or reprocessing of material or equipment as well as to material produced using U.S.-exported technology. These measures gave the United States much more control over the foreign uses of U.S.-origin nuclear material.

Title III of the NNPA includes such varied measures as requiring the Department of Energy to obtain NRC licenses to distribute source and special material and establishment of criteria for terminating nuclear exports from the United States (which affects bilateral nuclear cooperation agreements) to include detonation of a nuclear device, termination/abrogation or violation of IAEA safeguards, or engaging in activities involving nuclear material which have significance in the manufacture of nuclear explosive devices (covering a wide array of activities). Additional prohibited acts included violating a nuclear cooperation agreement with the United States; assisting a non-nuclear-weapon state in activities involving nuclear material that could potentially help in the manufacture or acquisition of a nuclear explosive device; or enriching any U.S. source

---

[37] This section drawn from CRS Report RL31502, *Nuclear, Biological, Chemical, and Missile Proliferation Sanctions: Selected Current Law*, by Dianne E. Rennack.

[38] P.L. 83-703, 42 U.S.C. 2011.

[39] P.L. 95-242, 22 U.S.C. 3201.

or special material without the permission of the United States. The NNPA requires (in Section 601) the President to report annually to Congress on the government's efforts to prevent nuclear proliferation.

The Arms Export Control Act (AECA)[40]

The Arms Export Control Act (AECA), as amended, authorizes U.S. government military sales, loans, leases, financing, and licensing of commercial arms sales to other countries. The AECA coordinates such actions with other foreign policy considerations, including nonproliferation, and determines eligibility of recipients for military exports, sales, leases, loans, and financing.

- *Section 3(f) (22 U.S.C. 2753(f))* prohibits U.S. military sales or leases to any country that the President determines is in material breach of binding commitments to the United States under international treaties or agreements regarding nonproliferation of nuclear explosive devices and unsafeguarded special nuclear material.

- *Section 40 (22 U.S.C. 2780)* prohibits exports or assistance in exporting (financial or otherwise) munitions to countries that provide support for terrorism. Included in the definition of acts of international terrorism are: "all activities that the Secretary [of State] determines willfully aid or abet the international proliferation of nuclear explosive devices to individuals or groups or willfully aid or abet an individual or groups in acquiring unsafeguarded special nuclear material." The President can rescind a determination or waive sanctions if essential to the national security interests of the United States.

- *Section 101 (22 U.S.C. 2799aa)* (formerly section 669 of the Foreign Assistance Act) prohibits foreign economic or military assistance to countries that deliver or receive nuclear enrichment equipment, materials, or technology unless the supplier agrees to place such under safeguards and the recipient has full-scope safeguards. The President, who makes the determination, can waive sanctions if they will have a serious adverse effect on vital U.S. interests, given assurances that the recipient will not acquire, develop, or assist others in acquiring or developing nuclear weapons.

- *Section 102 (22 U.S.C. 2799aa-1)* (formerly section 670 of the Foreign Assistance Act) prohibits foreign economic or military assistance to countries that deliver or receive nuclear reprocessing equipment, material, or technology to or from another country; or any non-nuclear-weapon state which illegally exports from the United States items that would contribute to nuclear proliferation. The President, who makes the determination, can waive the sanction if he finds that ending assistance would adversely affect U.S. nonproliferation objectives or jeopardize the common defense and security. The section further prohibits assistance (except humanitarian or food assistance), defense sales, export licenses for U.S. Munitions List items, other export licenses subject to foreign policy controls, and various credits and loans to any country that the President has

---

[40] P.L. 90-629, 22 U.S.C. 2751. Title 22 of the U.S. Code, Chapter 39, addresses Arms Export Control. Subchapter VII addresses control of missiles and missile exports or technology; subchapter VIII addresses chemical weapons and biological weapons, and subchapter X addresses nuclear nonproliferation controls.

determined transfers a nuclear explosive device, design information, or component to a non-nuclear-weapons state, or is a non-nuclear-weapons state and receives a nuclear device, design information, or component, or detonates a nuclear explosive device.

Much of the language on nuclear nonproliferation controls that had been incorporated into the Foreign Assistance Act earlier (including the 1977 Glenn-Symington amendments on enrichment and reprocessing and the 1985 Pressler amendment related to Pakistan) were incorporated into the AECA in 1994 by the Nuclear Proliferation Prevention Act (see discussion below).

Export Administration Act of 1979 (EAA)

The Export Administration Act of 1979 (P.L. 96-72) authorizes the executive branch to regulate private sector exports of particular goods and technology to other countries. Although the act expired in 1989, export controls have been implemented under executive orders and the International Emergency Economic Powers Act (IEEPA).[41] The EAA coordinates such actions with other foreign policy considerations, including nonproliferation, and determines eligibility of recipients for exports. *Section 5 (50 U.S.C. app. 2404)* authorizes the President to curtail or prohibit the export of any goods or services for national security reasons: to comply with other laws regarding a potential recipient country's political status or political stability, to cooperate with international agreements or understandings, or to protect militarily critical technologies. *Section 6 (50 U.S.C. app. 2405)* authorizes the President to curtail or prohibit the export of goods or services for foreign policy reasons. Within Section 6, for example, *Section 6(j)* establishes the State Department's list of countries found to be supporting acts of international terrorism, a list on which many other restrictions and prohibitions in law are based.

Export-Import Bank Act of 1945

The Export-Import Bank Act of 1945 (P.L. 79-173) establishes the Export-Import Bank of the United States and authorizes the Bank to finance and facilitate exports and imports and the exchange of commodities and services between the United States and foreign countries. Key nuclear-nonproliferation-related provisions were added in 1978. These include *Section 2(b)(1)(B) (12 U.S.C. 635(b)(1)(B))* and *Section 2(b)(4) (12 U.S.C. 635(b)(4))*, which together allow the Bank to deny credit generally if that credit does not help advance U.S. nuclear proliferation policy, and specifically, if a person or country has (1) violated, abrogated or terminated a nuclear safeguards agreements; (2) violated a nuclear cooperation agreement with the United States; or (3) aided or abetted a non-nuclear-weapon state to acquire a nuclear explosive device or to acquire unsafeguarded special nuclear material. There is a provision for presidential waiver. (See **Appendix B** for details.)

The Export-Import Bank Act of 1945 was amended in 2002[42] to allow denial of Ex-Im Bank financing for violations of the Foreign Corrupt Practices Act, the Arms Export Control Act, the International Emergency Economic Powers Act, or the Export Administration Act of 1979, extending its purview from strictly nuclear to CW, BW, and missile-related concerns.

---

[41] See CRS Report RL31832, *The Export Administration Act: Evolution, Provisions, and Debate*, by Ian F. Fergusson.

[42] See The Export-Import Bank Reauthorization Act of 2002, P.L. 107-189.

Nuclear Proliferation Prevention Act of 1994

In 1994 Congress approved the Nuclear Proliferation Prevention Act (NPPA, Title VIII, of the Foreign Relations Authorization Act, Fiscal Years 1994 and 1995, P.L. 103-236), which primarily strengthened penalties against persons who aid or abet the acquisition of nuclear weapons or unsafeguarded nuclear weapons materials, or countries (non-nuclear-weapon states) that obtain or explode nuclear devices. Sanctions include cutoff of U.S. assistance, prohibition on involvement with U.S. government procurement, stringent licensing requirements for technology exports, and opposition to loans or credits from international financial institutions. These sanctions were imposed on India and Pakistan following their nuclear tests in May 1998, but were gradually relaxed. Legislation passed in the 106th Congress extended the President's authority to relax sanctions on India and Pakistan for a year, and the Senate passed a bill suspending sanctions on the two countries for five years. The FY2000 Department of Defense Appropriations bill (P.L. 106-79) extended the authority to suspend sanctions. Following the September 11 terrorist attacks, President Bush lifted all remaining sanctions on India and Pakistan in response to support of U.S. operations in Afghanistan.

The NPPA defined for the first time in U.S. law the term "nuclear explosive device." It defined "terrorism" as used in the AECA, to include activities that assist groups or individuals to acquire any nuclear explosive device. It included a sense of Congress that identified 24 measures to strengthen IAEA safeguards, some of which have been implemented. Relevant sections include *Section 821 (22 U.S.C. 3201 note)*, which requires U.S. government procurement sanctions; *Section 823 (22 U.S.C. 3201 note)*, which requires U.S. executive directors of international financial institutions to vote against finance that might promote nuclear proliferation; and *Section 824 (22 U.S.C. 3201 note)*, which takes aim at financial institutions and persons involved with financial institutions from assisting nuclear proliferation through the provision of financing. (See **Appendix B** for specific details.)

Nunn-Lugar/Cooperative Threat Reduction Program Legislation

In late 1991, Congress passed the Soviet Nuclear Threat Reduction Act (which became known as the Nunn-Lugar Amendment), establishing programs to assist with the safe and secure storage and dismantlement of nuclear weapons in Russia and the Newly Independent States (NIS). These programs initially focused on the "loose nukes" problem, but have broadened their focus to address a variety of proliferation risks associated with weak political control over nuclear materials, equipment, and expertise, as well as CW, BW, and missiles. This effort has expanded to include the CTR program in DOD and nonproliferation programs in DOE and the State Department.[43] The FY2008 defense authorization bill expanded the program to countries outside the former Soviet Union, and eliminated the annual certification requirements for the CTR program.[44]

---

[43] See CRS Report 97-1027, *Nunn-Lugar Cooperative Threat Reduction Programs: Issues for Congress*, by Amy F. Woolf.

[44] See CRS Report RL31957, *Nonproliferation and Threat Reduction Assistance: U.S. Programs in the Former Soviet Union*, by Amy F. Woolf.

Iran-Iraq Arms Nonproliferation Act of 1992

Section 1602 of the Defense Authorization for FY1993 (Title XVI, P.L. 102-484, as amended) extended existing sanctions on Iraq to Iran. The law states that it is the policy of the United States to oppose any transfer to Iran or Iraq that could contribute to either country's ability to acquire nuclear, chemical, biological, or advanced conventional weapons. *Section 1604* requires the President to impose sanctions against any person whom he has determined to be engaged in such transfers. *Section 1605* similarly addresses activities of foreign governments. The 104th Congress amended the law (by passage of section 1408(a), P.L. 104-106, National Defense Authorization Act for Fiscal Year 1996) to make it apply to transfers contributing to the development of weapons of mass destruction as well as advanced conventional weapons.

Iran, North Korea and Syria Nonproliferation Act

The law (P.L. 106-178) imposes penalties on countries whose companies help Iran's efforts to acquire weapons of mass destruction and missile delivery systems. In 2005, P.L. 109-112, Iran Nonproliferation Amendments Act, added Syria to the law and added sanctions for transfers to and from those countries. In 2006, Congress also added North Korea to the Act (P.L. 109-353).

Foreign Operations, Export Financing, and Related Programs Appropriations Act of 2006

This law (P.L. 109-102) withheld 60% of funds set aside for assistance to the Russian government until the President certifies that assistance to Iran has ceased. Assistance constitutes technical training, expertise, technology, or equipment needed to build a nuclear reactor, develop research facilities or programs, or ballistic missile technologies.

Issues for the 111th Congress

Since September 11, 2001, much of Congress's attention in the area of the nonproliferation of weapons of mass destruction has focused on how to mitigate the threat U.S. citizens face right now—improving domestic preparedness against WMD terrorism and improving intelligence capabilities to detect evidence of proliferation-related activities. Above all, however, most experts agree that the U.S. government should continue to address nuclear proliferation at the source— that is, securing nuclear materials and halting information flows from WMD-knowledgeable scientists to countries of proliferation concern.

Other key nuclear nonproliferation issues for Congress include:

- facilitating implementation of DOD's Cooperative Threat Reduction and relevant DOE programs that improve controls on nuclear materials, equipment, and expertise in Russia and the NIS and expanding these efforts to countries outside the NIS;

- monitoring efforts to end Pyongyang's nuclear weapons program;

- monitoring Iran's nuclear program, including Russian and Chinese nuclear exports and assistance;

- opposing the nuclear arms race between India and Pakistan, preventing those countries from exporting WMD technology and cooperating to prevent terrorist access to their facilities;

- strengthening the IAEA safeguards system to enforce the NPT and prevent further proliferation;

- maintaining and expanding adherence to NSG nuclear export control standards;

- curbing dangerous Chinese and Russian nuclear exports;

- banning the production of fissile material for nuclear weapons;

- consideration of the future of the U.S. nuclear arsenal and impact of these policies on nonproliferation.

Closer to home, Congress will be asked to consider how to dispose of tons of excess plutonium from dismantled Russian and U.S. warheads without increasing proliferation risks; and how U.S. arms control and defense cooperation (particularly missile defense cooperation) might affect proliferation risks. Congress will also be asked to assess U.S. and multilateral programs to lessen the proliferation risks of an expansion of nuclear energy. Congress may also exert oversight over key nonproliferation programs, such as Proliferation Security Initiative and the Global Threat Reduction Initiative.

Chemical and Biological Weapons Proliferation Regime[45]

Prohibitions against the use of chemical weapons date back to the International Peace Conferences that met at the Hague in 1899 and 1907; these pre-World War I prohibitions were reaffirmed in the 1919 Versailles Treaty and further expanded in the 1925 Geneva Protocol. In some ways, it is more difficult to prevent the proliferation of these weapons than nuclear weapons because they require a smaller infrastructure and the production technologies are much more widely disseminated. Furthermore, it is more difficult to distinguish between legitimate and illegitimate chemical and biological activities.[46] The regimes that have grown up around these weapons include treaties, supplier agreements, and domestic laws.

Treaties and Agreements

The Chemical Weapons Convention (CWC) and the Biological and Toxin Weapons Convention (BWC) are the two primary treaties related to CBW proliferation. The United States is a state party to both the BWC and the CWC.

---

[45] This section was prepared by Paul Kerr.

[46] United Nations Institute for Disarmament Research, "Blood, Toil, Tears and Sweat: The Biological and Toxin Weapons Convention since 2001," *Disarmament Forum*, 2006.

Chemical Weapons Convention (CWC)

Culminating 25 years of negotiations, the Chemical Weapons Convention opened for signature in January 1993.[47] The CWC entered into force on April 29, 1997. As of January 27, 2010, the treaty had 188 states-parties.[48]

The CWC prohibits the development, production, stockpiling, transfer, and use of chemical weapons. The convention mandates the destruction of chemical weapon arsenals within 10 years of its coming into force. The CWC also restricts the international transfer of chemicals deemed useful in the production of chemical weapons, so-called "precursors." Most precursor chemicals are dual-use, with legitimate peaceful applications. The CWC establishes extensive lists or "schedules" of precursors whose production, use, and transfer must be reported to the CWC's Organization for the Prohibition of Chemical Weapons (OPCW). The schedules are designated I-III, in order of their potential usefulness in chemical warfare. Schedule I chemicals may be exported only to states parties (i.e., nations that have ratified the CWC). In accordance with treaty provisions, as of April 2000, the export of Schedule II chemicals to non-states parties became prohibited.

Biological and Toxin Weapons Convention

The Biological Weapons Convention was concluded in 1972, with U.S. ratification and entry in force in 1975.[49] As of January 27, 2010, the convention had 163 states parties. The convention bans the development, production, and stockpiling of biological agents or toxins "of types and in quantities that have no justification for peaceful purposes." The development, manufacture, and possession of BW weapons or delivery systems is also prohibited. States parties also agree not to transfer biological agents or toxins for any but peaceful purposes.[50]

The United Kingdom first tabled a draft treaty in 1968 that contained verification provisions. Assuming the Soviet Union would reject such a proposal, the United States, with UK agreement, privately negotiated a treaty text with the Soviets that did not include a verification mechanism. On the same day in 1969, both the United States and the Soviet Union tabled identical draft treaties. In 1969, the United States declared a unilateral end to its offensive BW program and suggested separating the BW issue from the chemical-biological arms control negotiations in Geneva. Negotiations on this proposal took three years to conclude.

Implementing the Regime

International Organizations

The CBW nonproliferation regime relies on the Australia Group and the Organization for the Prohibition of Chemical Weapons (OPCW), which was created by the CWC. There is no

---

[47] http://www.opcw.org.

[48] For more information about the CWC's status, see CRS Report RL 33865, *Arms Control and Nonproliferation: A Catalog of Treaties and Agreements,* by Amy F. Woolf, Mary Beth Nikitin, and Paul K Kerr.

[49] http://www.fas.org/nuke/control/bwc/text/bwc.htm.

[50] For more information about the BWC's status, see CRS Report RL 33865.

independent international organization to administer the Biological Weapons Convention. Currently, BWC member states report all defensive biological activities to the United Nations Department of Disarmament Affairs. This information is reported to all BWC member states, with the State Department as the international point of contact within the U.S. government. The states-parties decided in December 2006 to establish an Implementation Support Unit for the BWC. According to its website, the three-person unit provides "administrative support and assistance; National Implementation support and assistance; Support and assistance for Confidence-Building Measures; and Support and assistance for obtaining universality."[51]

Australia Group (AG)

In 1984, United Nations investigators officially confirmed that chemical weapons had been used in the Iran-Iraq War. In response, the United States and several other countries began to implement export controls on chemicals that could be used to manufacture chemical weapons. In 1985, Australia proposed that concerned countries meet in order to coordinate their export controls and share information to enhance their effectiveness. The first meeting took place in June 1985, and biennial meetings continue at the Australian embassy in Paris.

The Australia Group has established a list of chemicals and equipment that are subject to control. In 1990, in response to growing concerns over the proliferation of covert biological weapons programs, certain biological agents and research/production equipment were added to the control list. Australia Group guidelines do not call for prohibiting the export of control list items, but rather establishing monitoring and licensing procedures, with export denial only if there is reason to suspect potential contribution to a CBW program. The group's list does not curtail legitimate trade. Since its inception, the Australia Group has added controls on the transfer of information and knowledge that could aid BW proliferation. These included "catch-all" constraints covering items that are not on control lists, adding eight toxins to the control list, adopting controls on technology associated with dual-use biological equipment, and agreeing to control intangible technology transfer (i.e., by phone, fax, or internet) that could be used to advance CBW programs.

As noted, the Australia Group does not have an independent administrative organization. National governments administer their own export control programs. As an informal effort, it is not based on international treaty, is not affiliated with any international organization, and has no independent administrative structure. It operates entirely upon consensus of its 41 members and its decisions are not binding. Countries are admitted to membership only upon the full consensus of current members, and must have demonstrated compliance with the CWC and BWC, and have an effective export control regime.

The question of the Australia Group's relationship to the Chemical Weapons Convention revolves around the convention's Article XI which declares that states parties will not

> maintain among themselves any restrictions, including those in any international agreements, incompatible with the obligations undertaken under this Convention, which would restrict or impede trade and the development and promotion of scientific and technological knowledge.

---

[51] http://www.unog.ch/80256EE600585943/(httpPages)/16C37624830EDAE5C12572BC0044DFC1?OpenDocument.

The Australia Group maintains that its export control regime is compatible with the objectives of the convention, and therefore not prohibited. A number of developing countries, led by Iran (a CWC state party), maintain that the AG controls should be dropped—particularly for CWC states parties. They view the controls as a tool of economic oppression on the part of developed countries, even though no country has been able to provide an example where AG controls have resulted in a denial of exports for legitimate purposes.

Organization for the Prohibition of Chemical Weapons (OPCW)

The OPCW is headquartered in The Hague. It has four components:

- Conference of States Parties—Comprises all nations who have ratified the convention; meets annually; has the responsibility to ensure compliance and levy sanctions; selects the Executive Council;

- Executive Council—Comprises 41 states parties on a two-year rotation[52]; directs the routine administration of the OPCW;

- Technical Secretariat—Comprises a permanent international work force; administers and monitors treaty compliance (inspections, data collection and assessment);

- Scientific Advisory Board—Comprised of independent experts to advise the OPCW on relevant scientific and technical issues.

U.S. Government Organizations

In the United States, the following offices, among others, participate in administering the CBW export control program, with State serving as the international point of contact:

- Department of Commerce—Under Secretary of Commerce, Bureau of Industry and Security;

- Department of State—Under Secretary for Arms Control and International Security—Bureau of International Security and Nonproliferation administers the CWC and export controls;

- Department of Defense—Deputy Under Secretary for Technology Security Policy and Counterproliferation;

- The Department of the Treasury oversees U.S. embargoes through its Office of Foreign Assets Control;

- The Department of Homeland Security enforces export control through the U.S. Customs Service.

---

[52] By virtue of the treaty-prescribed method of selecting rotational members, the United States will always have a seat on the Executive Council.

U.S. Laws[53]

U.S. laws pertaining to chemical and biological weapons proliferation include statutes and executive orders, the most important of which are the Export Administration Act and the Arms Export Control Act. These statutes operate on the principle that licenses are required for the export of certain goods, and that it is government policy to deny such licenses if there is a danger that the items will contribute to CBW proliferation.

Export Administration Act of 1979

(P.L. 96-72, Section 6(m) and 11C, 50 U.S.C. App. 2405m and 2410c). This act requires a license for the export of dual-use goods or technology that "would directly and substantially" assist CBW proliferation. Under the act, the Secretary of Commerce maintains a list of such goods. Exports to countries which have entered into an agreement for the control of restricted goods (i.e., Australia Group members) are exempted from licensing requirements. The EAA requires the President to impose procurement and import sanctions on foreign persons who contribute to CBW proliferation through exports.

Arms Export Control Act

Section 81 of the AECA (22 U.S.C. 2798) provides the State Department the authority to maintain licensing of the export of chemical and biological agents and munitions. It also provides criminal penalties for violation and specifies sanctions against foreign persons who contribute to CW or BW proliferation through exports, and against countries which use chemical or biological weapons or make substantial preparations to do so.

Chemical and Biological Weapons Control and Warfare Elimination Act of 1991[54]

This act mandates U.S. sanctions, and encourages international sanctions, against countries that use chemical or biological weapons in violation of international law. *Section 307 (22 U.S.C. 5605)* requires the President to terminate foreign assistance (except humanitarian, food, and agricultural assistance) arms sales and licenses, credits, guarantees, and certain exports to a government of a foreign country that he has determined has used or made substantial preparation to use chemical or biological weapons. Within three months, the President must determine and certify to Congress that the government: is no longer using chemical or biological weapons in violation of international law, is no longer using such weapons against its own people, has provided credible assurances that such behavior will not resume, and is willing to cooperate with U.N. or other international observers to verify that biological and chemical weapons are not still in use. Without this three-month determination, sanctions are required affecting multilateral development bank loans, U.S. bank loans or credits, exports, imports, diplomatic relations, and aviation access to and from the United States. The President may lift the sanctions after a year, and may waive the imposition of these sanctions.

---

[53] This section drawn from CRS Report RL31502, *Nuclear, Biological, Chemical, and Missile Proliferation Sanctions: Selected Current Law*, by Dianne E. Rennack.

[54] Title III, P.L. 102-182, 22 U.S.C. 5601-5606.

Biological Anti-Terrorism Act of 1989

This act (P.L. 101-298) implements the Biological Weapons Convention, providing criminal penalties for its violation. It does not amend either the Export Administration Act or the Arms Export Control Act.

Additional CW/BW Nonproliferation Policy Provisions in Legislation

Congress has expressed views on CW/BW nonproliferation policy and U.S. government organization to implement those policies in several other laws. CBW-related provisions have been included in the Iran-Iraq Arms Nonproliferation Act of 1992, the Freedom Support Act, and the Cooperative Threat Reduction Act. These and other provisions are listed in **Table 2**.

Issues for the 111th Congress

Export Controls

Effective export controls are generally viewed as critical tools to stem the proliferation of chemical and biological weapons. The 111th Congress may consider changes to the export control laws. For example, on July 31, 2009, Representative Sherman introduced the Export Control Improvements Act (H.R. 3515), co-sponsored by Representative Manzullo and Representative A. Smith, which contains provisions on export controls enforcement, integration of export control data in the AES, and diversion control.[55] In addition, the White House announced in August 2009 that it was beginning a "broad-based interagency process for reviewing the overall U.S. export control system." When evaluating proposals for changing export controls, Congress may consider potential implications for the multilateral proliferation control regimes.

U.S. Compliance With CWC

None of the six CWC states-parties that declared possession of chemical weapons destroyed their stocks by the original April 29, 2007, deadline. In July 2007, Albania became the first country to have destroyed its declared chemical weapons. South Korea became the second on July 10, 2008. India became the third on March 16, 2009. Three other states—Libya, Russia, and the United States—have declared possession of such weapons and all three have stated their intentions to destroy them.

The United States has already destroyed all of its Category Three stockpile and has declared no Category Two weapons. However, it has encountered difficulties in destroying its Category One chemical weapons stockpile. In April 2006, the United States submitted a formal request to the OPCW chairman and director-general to extend Washington's final chemical weapons destruction deadline from April 2007 to April 29, 2012, the latest possible date allowed under the CWC.[56]

---

[55] Taken from CRS Report RL 31832, *The Export Administration Act: Evolution, Provisions, and Debate*, by Ian F. Fergusson. See that report for more information on the proposed legislation.

[56] Ambassador Eric Javits, U.S. Permanent Representative to the OPCW, Statement Concerning Request to Extend the United States' Destruction Deadline Under the Chemical Weapons Convention, April 20, 2006. Available at http://www.state.gov/t/isn/rls/rm/64878 htm.

However, Ambassador Eric Javits, U.S. Permanent Representative to the OPCW, added that "we do not expect to be able to meet that deadline" because Washington had encountered "delays and difficulties" in destroying its stockpile.[57] These delays have generally resulted from the need to meet state and federal environmental requirements and from both local and congressional concerns over the means of destruction.

Reinforcing Javits' statement, former Secretary of Defense Donald Rumsfeld notified Congress in April 2006 that destruction of the U.S. stockpile by the April 2012 deadline "was in doubt based on the current schedules, but that the Department of Defense [DOD] would continue requesting resources needed to complete destruction as close to the 2012 deadline as practicable."

Andrew Weber, Assistant Secretary of Defense for Nuclear and Chemical and Biological Defense Programs, told the OPCW November 30, 2009, that the United States has destroyed over 67% of its Category One stockpile.[58] Washington projects that its four operating destruction facilities[59] will have destroyed 90% of the total U.S. stockpile by 2017.[60] Two other facilities under construction will destroy the remaining chemical agents stockpiles located at Pueblo, CO, and Lexington, KY. A 2007 estimate from the DOD Assembled Chemical Weapons Alternatives (ACWA) program stated that these stockpiles would be destroyed by 2020 and 2023, respectively.[61]

However, the 2008 Defense Appropriations Act (P.L. 110-116) required the Defense Department to "complete work on the destruction" of the U.S. chemical weapons stockpile by the 2012 deadline "and in no circumstances later than December 31, 2017." Additionally, the National Defense Authorization Act for Fiscal Year 2008 (P.L. 110-181) required that the Secretary of Defense submit a report to Congress that includes a

> description of the options and alternatives for accelerating the completion of chemical weapons destruction at each such facility, particularly in time to meet the [CWC] destruction deadline of April 29, 2012 ... and by December 31, 2017.

That report, submitted in June 2008, compared three options for accelerating stockpile destruction, noting that "[t]here are no options to achieve 100 percent destruction of the national stockpile by 2012."[62] The three options were as follows:

- Provide schedule incentives authorized by Congress[63] to ensure that the operating sites complete the destruction of their stockpiles by 2012.

- Transport portions of the remaining stockpile to destruction facilities that are already operating.

- Accelerate the destruction schedule for the Colorado and Kentucky sites.

---

[57] *Ibid.*

[58] The United States has destroyed all of its chemical weapons munitions.

[59] These sites are managed by the U.S. Army Chemical Materials Agency (CMA). The facilities under construction in Colorado and Kentucky are managed by the Assembled Chemical Weapons Alternatives program.

[60] Department of Defense Report *Chemical Demilitarization Program Semi-Annual Report to Congress,* May 2009.

[61] See ACWA Cost and Schedule Information. Available at http://www.pmacwa.army.mil/ip/dl/ acwa_cost_schedule.pdf

[62] *Chemical Demilitarization Program Semi-Annual Report to Congress,* 2008.

[63] In section 923 of P.L. 109-364.

A May 2009 DOD report to Congress proposes that the Department "seek additional resources" to complete destruction of the Colorado stockpile by 2017 and the Kentucky stockpile by 2021.[64] The 2010 Department of Defense Appropriations Act enables the Department to meet this timetable.[65]

U.S. Funding for OPCW

Ambassador Robert Mikulak stated April 20, 2010, that earlier that month Washington had "authorized full payment of the outstanding balance of our 2010 assessed contribution to the OPCW," explaining that the United States had previously "split our payment: 30% of our assessment in the first part of the year and the remaining 70% in the last three months. However, we have now been able to regularize our payment schedule so that our full assessment can be paid in the first part of the year."

Some observers had argued that, because the U.S. assessment comprises a large percentage of the OPCW's budget, these late payments negatively affected the organization's financial planning. Moreover, the Conference of States Parties Convention recognized the "negative consequences of the late payment of assessed contributions on the operational activities" of the OCPW in a December 2009 statement.[66]

Biological Weapons Convention — U.S. Biodefense Programs

In conducting oversight, the 111th Congress may consider the issue of transparency in U.S. biodefense programs. Some observers have argued that these programs could create suspicions that the United States is conducting research related to biological weapons that is prohibited by the BWC.[67]

Missile Proliferation Control Regime[68]

In the early 1980s, the United States and its allies heightened their concern over the spread of missiles as the advanced industrial nations' monopoly on missile technology gave way to a diffusion of missiles and missile technology throughout much of the world. In April 1987, the United States, Canada, France, West Germany, Italy, Japan, and the United Kingdom created the Missile Technology Control Regime (MTCR) to prevent the proliferation of missiles and unmanned aerial vehicles capable of delivering nuclear weapons. Today, 34 countries are formal

---

[64] *Chemical Demilitarization Program Semi-Annual Report to Congress,* 2009.

[65] Analyst interview with ACWA official, January 28, 2010.

[66] Decision Programme and Budget of the OPCW for 2010, December 2, 2009, C-14/DEC.8.

[67] CRS Report RL32891, *The National Biodefense Analysis and Countermeasures Center: Issues for Congress,* by Dana A. Shea. See also, Jonathan Tucker, "Seeking Biosecurity Without Verification: The New U.S. Strategy on Biothreats," *Arms Control Today,* January/February 2010.

[68] This section was prepared by Steven A. Hildreth.

---

partners in the MTCR.[69] Although there is no permanent secretariat or headquarters, the French Foreign Ministry acts as a central point of contact.

In addition, China, Israel, Romania, and the Slovak Republic have agreed to observe MTCR guidelines as "unilateral adherents." China's application for MTCR membership, submitted in 2004, remains under review by the MTCR member states. China officially reiterated its commitment to MTCR goals in February 2008. Israel completed a memorandum of understanding with the United States affirming its commitment to abide by MTCR guidelines. Under the U.S.-India nuclear agreement (U.S.-India 123 Agreement of October 2008), India will be required to adhere to MTCR guidelines. And in April 2009, Kazakhstan said it would consider joining the MTCR a foreign policy priority.

The regime is based on the premise that foreign acquisition and development of missiles can be delayed, made more difficult and expensive, and even prevented if major producers agree to control exports of missiles and the equipment and technology used in missile production. The MTCR is similar in this regard to the Nuclear Suppliers Group, the Australia Group, and the Wassenaar Arrangement. It differs from the nuclear and chemical non-proliferation regimes in that the MTCR is not supported by a treaty and has no international organization to verify or enforce compliance. Rather, the MTCR is a set of common export control guidelines adopted and administered independently by each of the partner nations through consensus.

The specific missile equipment and technology subject to the guidelines is described in an annex to the MTCR Guidelines and divided into two categories. Each of the member countries is to exercise particular restraint in considering transfers of items in Category I, which include complete rocket systems and unmanned air vehicle (UAV) systems capable of delivering a 500-kilogram (1,100-pound) payload to a range of 300 kilometers (186 miles) or more, and complete subsystems of such missiles and vehicles. There is a strong presumption by the MTCR to deny transfers of these systems and components. The guidelines further state that the transfer of Category I production facilities will not be authorized.

In addition, export restraints are to be applied to Category II items, which consist of other components, equipment, material, and technology that would be usable in the production of missiles and UAVs. Category II also includes, at item number 19, complete rocket systems and UAVs with a 300-km range but not capable of delivering a 500-kg payload to that range (as covered by Category I), and in item number 20, individual rocket stages and rocket engines and production equipment usable for systems with a range of 300 km with less than a 500-kg payload.

In January 1993, MTCR partners revised the guidelines to limit the risks of proliferation of missile delivery systems for all weapons of mass destruction: chemical and biological weapons as well as nuclear weapons. The guidelines now call for particular restraint and the presumption to deny transfers of any missiles (whether or not they are included in the annex) and of any items in the annex if the government judges that they are intended to be used for the delivery of weapons of mass destruction.[70] This addition is commonly referred to as a "catch-all" clause.

---

[69] See **Appendix A** for a list of current partners.

[70] According to the guidelines, the government judgment on the likely use of the missile items will be made, "on the basis of all available, persuasive information, evaluated according to factors including:

A. Concerns about the proliferation of weapons of mass destruction;

B. The capabilities and objectives of the missile and space programs of the recipient state;

(continued...)

The MTCR has undergone a transformation from a small group of Western industrial countries to a more inclusive formal and informal group of countries. Argentina, with its Condor II missile program, was originally one of the primary targets of the regime, but that country terminated development of Condor II and is now a full partner in the MTCR. South Africa and Brazil had active missile programs but are now partners. Brazil currently chairs the MTCR. Whereas the Soviet Union was the primary source for missiles to the Third World in the 1970s and 1980s, Russia has become a partner in the MTCR. Even so, the United States has sanctioned some Russian organizations for improper exports to Iran. China has been, and still is, another significant supplier of missiles and missile technology to developing countries, but has committed to observing the MTCR guidelines and pledged not to transfer surface-to-surface missiles that meet the MTCR thresholds. In spite of these commitments, some Russian and Chinese organizations and individuals apparently continue to supply components and technical assistance for missile production.

North Korea reportedly has become a primary supplier of missiles and missile technology to some developing countries. Iran, Syria, India, and Pakistan are the other countries of major concern regarding the development and acquisition of missiles. Missile programs in China, Egypt, and South Korea have also caused concern in Washington. Cruise missiles have always been included with ballistic missiles and space-launch vehicles in the MTCR but are now receiving greater attention as advanced propulsion and guidance technology is becoming more widely available.

The United States long ago stated its support for expanding membership of the MTCR "to include additional countries that subscribe to international non-proliferation standards, enforce effective export controls, and abandon offensive ballistic missile programs."[71] The United States will not support space launch programs in non-MTCR countries, but will consider exports of MTCR items for use in space-launch programs by MTCR countries on a case-by-case basis. The United States and other MTCR countries are promoting regional efforts to reduce the demand for missiles and persuade countries to forgo the acquisition of missiles.

Some nations have not joined the MTCR, affirming their sovereign right to acquire, develop, deploy, and export missiles. It has been particularly difficult to control dual-use technologies that may be used for civilian space launch vehicles, civil aviation, general industry, and tactical weapons.

MTCR member states have been working since about 1999 on a supplementary effort that has become known as the International Code of Conduct (ICOC) Against Ballistic Missile Proliferation. On November 25, 2002, the ICOC entered into force and the United States was an initial subscribing member. The code includes broad principles, general commitments and modest confidence-building measures. The Bush Administration saw the ICOC as "an important addition to the wide range of tools available to countries to impede and roll back this proliferation

---

(...continued)

C. The significance of the transfer in terms of the potential development of delivery systems (other than manned aircraft) for weapons of mass destruction;

D. The assessment of the end-use of the transfers, including the relevant assurances of the recipient states ... ; and

E. The applicability of relevant multilateral agreements."

[71] U.S. Department of State, Reprint of White House Press Release, *Non-Proliferation and Export Control Policy*, September 27, 1993.

threat."[72] The code attempts to fill the gap of demand-side incentives by offering "cooperation" with respect to civilian space-launch vehicle technology in exchange for significant nonproliferation commitments. However, such cooperation is to be worked out between states and is not specified in the draft document, making incentives for cooperation appear a bit elusive.

Implementing the Regime

International Organization

Although the MTCR has no international organization, partner countries hold monthly meetings in Paris among embassy representatives (called "points of contact" meetings), hold technical experts' meetings (including information exchanges) and convene a plenary once each year. In this manner, partners revise the guidelines and the equipment annex and admit new partners. At the Madrid 2005 Plenary, partners emphasized that the threat of proliferation of WMD delivery systems constitutes a threat to international peace and security and stressed the need to reduce the risks associated with terrorism in this regard. This theme has been reiterated each year since.

U.S. Government Organization

The Directorate of Defense Trade Controls of the State Department administers the regulations governing the export of items on the Munitions List—those items that are subject to controls under the AECA and the ITAR.[73] The Bureau of Industry and Security in the U.S. Department of Commerce administers the regulations governing the export of items on the Commerce Control List—those items that are primarily for civilian use but have applications for the development, testing, or production of missiles.[74]

The Missile Technology Export Control (MTEC) working group is chaired by a State Department official that reviews controversial missile export license cases. The Missile Trade Analysis Group (MTAG), another interagency group chaired by a State Department representative, reviews intelligence reports on diversions of missile technology from legitimate recipients to others.[75]

Officials in the State Department's Bureau of International Security and Nonproliferation (ISN) and regional bureaus also undertake diplomatic initiatives to dissuade additional nations from developing missiles, to persuade other countries to adopt export controls on missile technology, and to reduce the perceived need for missiles.[76]

Department of Defense officials have established a counter-proliferation policy that addresses export controls, security relationships with friendly and hostile countries, defensive and offensive military operational concepts, and equipment. Many organizations within the Department implement the various aspects of the counter-proliferation policy, but the Assistant Secretary for

---

[72] John R. Bolton, Remarks at the Launching Conference for the ICOC, The Hague, The Netherlands, November 25, 2002. See http://www.state.gov/t/us/rm/15488.htm.

[73] http://www.pmddtc.state.gov

[74] http://www.bis.doc.gov

[75] http://www.state.gov/t/isn/58386.htm

[76] http://www.state.gov/t/isn

International Security Policy (ASD(ISP)) has the primary responsibility for counter-proliferation policy formulation.[77]

The Department of the Treasury also oversees U.S. embargoes through its Office of Foreign Assets Control (OFAC), and helps enforce export controls through the U.S. Customs Service.[78]

U.S. Laws[79]

The United States has maintained stringent controls on missiles and missile technology under the Arms Export Control Act (22 U.S.C. 2751) and the International Traffic in Arms Regulations (22 C.F.R. Part 121, hereafter the ITAR).

In the early 1980s, the United States also unilaterally adopted tighter export controls on dual-use equipment and technology that could benefit foreign missile programs. Dual-use controls have been placed in the Export Administration Regulations (15 C.F.R. 730-799) pursuant to the authority of the Export Administration Act of 1979 (50 U.S.C. app. 2401 et seq.) and the International Emergency Economic Powers Act (50 U.S.C. 1701 et seq.). Successive administrations have updated regulations to reflect changes adopted by the MTCR, changes in U.S. law, and the changing international political environment. The Export Administration Act of 1979 has expired several times, but the President has invoked his authority to continue in effect the system of controls that had been maintained under the act.

Members of Congress became concerned about missile proliferation in the mid-1980s because growing evidence of missile proliferation in developing world was an additional consideration in funding President Reagan's ballistic missile defense programs. Libya had purchased Soviet Scud missiles and Iran and Iraq were firing missiles at each other. Congress had little or no involvement in shaping the MTCR, because it was neither a treaty nor an executive agreement. Soon after the regime was announced in April 1987, it became apparent that companies and individuals from a number of MTCR member countries (such as West Germany, Italy, Britain, and France) had transferred goods and technical assistance to missile development teams in Argentina, Brazil, Iraq, Egypt, and elsewhere. In 1987, the United States also learned that China had transferred intermediate range missiles to Saudi Arabia. Many Members of Congress thought the MTCR needed enforcement mechanisms, additional members, and stricter compliance.

Several bills were introduced at the time with the intention of strengthening the U.S. position on missile nonproliferation. Those bills that included sanctions against nations, companies, and individuals who violate the MTCR guidelines gained widespread bipartisan congressional support. At the time, Bush Administration officials maintained that the President already had sufficient authority to reprimand or sanction foreign governments, companies, and individuals for inappropriate missile transfers and objected to the imposition of mandatory statutory sanctions. President George H.W. Bush pocket-vetoed the Export Administration Act of 1990, which included a missile nonproliferation provision, as well as the Chemical and Biological Weapons Control Act. However, he signed the defense authorization bill that contained a nearly identical section on missile nonproliferation policy.

---

[77] http://www.fas.org/irp/doddir/dod/ds111_14.pdf

[78] http://www.treas.gov.offices/enforcement/ofac

[79] This section drawn from CRS Report RL31502, *Nuclear, Biological, Chemical, and Missile Proliferation Sanctions: Selected Current Law*, by Dianne E. Rennack.

The Missile Technology Control Act of 1990

The act became law in the 101st Congress (H.R. 4739, Title XVII of the National Defense Authorization Act for Fiscal Year 1991, P.L. 101-510). It added Chapter 7 to the Arms Export Control Act, sections 6(l) and 11B to the Export Administration Act of 1979, and established an annual reporting requirement. Chapter 7 of the AECA has been amended several times.

The Arms Export Control Act

(22 U.S.C. 2751 et seq.) Chapter 7 of the AECA requires the President to impose sanctions on U.S. and foreign individuals who improperly conduct trade in controlled missile technology. If someone inappropriately transfers MTCR Category II goods or technology, they will be denied, for two years, any U.S. government contracts relating to missile equipment or technology, and U.S. export licenses for missile equipment and technology. The AECA requires sanctions for at least two years if a person inappropriately transfers Category I items; these include denial of all U.S. government contracts and export licenses for any item on the U.S. Munitions List. If the President determines that a foreign person has substantially contributed to the design, development, or production of missiles by a non-MTCR country, he shall prohibit for at least two years U.S. imports of items produced by that person. The act includes presidential waivers, exclusions, determination requirements, and definitions that allow the Administration to take no action in certain circumstances.

These sanctions may be waived by the President, and they generally do not apply to transfers of missile goods or technology to an MTCR adherent or from an MTCR adherent. The United States has imposed missile sanctions against entities in several countries including China, Pakistan, South Africa, North Korea, Iran, Russia, India, Syria, and Egypt.

The Export Administration Act of 1979

(Sections 6 (l) and 11B, 50 U.S.C. app. 2405 and app. 2410b). Similarly, the EAA requires controls on U.S. missile-related exports and sanctions against U.S. and foreign persons who improperly transfer dual-use goods or technology listed in the MTCR annex. If a person improperly transfers Category II goods or technology, he will be denied export licenses for two years for missile equipment and technology controlled under the EAA. If a person improperly exports Category I goods or technology, he will be denied export licenses for at least two years for all items controlled under the EAA. If a foreign person exports goods or technology that substantially contribute to the design, development, or production of missiles in a non-MTCR country, he will be denied license to import his products into the United States for at least two years. Actions that trigger sanctions under the provisions of either the AECA or the EAA, require commensurate sanctions under the other act.

Additional Missile Nonproliferation Policy Provisions in Legislation

Over the years, Congress has called for additional sanctions, expressed views to strengthen nonproliferation policies related to missiles or advanced conventional weapons, and expressed views on improving the organization of the U.S. government to implement those policies in several other laws. There are provisions related to missile proliferation in the Foreign Assistance Act of 1961, the Iran, North Korea and Syria Nonproliferation Act, the Iran-Iraq Arms

Nonproliferation Act of 1992, the Freedom Support Act, and the Cooperative Threat Reduction Act. These and other laws are listed in **Appendix B**.

Issues for the 111th Congress

A perennial issue of varying interest is whether the MTCR and the associated U.S. sanctions are effective enough to warrant the economic and political costs to the United States, and whether additional or alternative feasible measures would increase effectiveness.

Many analysts consider the MTCR a successful vehicle for quiet diplomacy. The MTCR has been credited with slowing missile development in Brazil and India, and blocking a collaborative program of Argentina, Egypt, and Iraq to build the Condor missile. This missile would have been a significant improvement over the Scud-based missiles used by Iraq in the Gulf War. Russia and China have probably stopped exporting entire missiles that fall under the parameters of the MTCR, even though some entities within those countries may continue to transfer components and technology. Most European countries and Asian allies have tightened their export control laws and some have prosecuted individuals who have smuggled missile technology as well as nuclear and chemical production technology. Long-range ballistic missiles are expensive and extraordinarily difficult to develop and produce. Because most countries cannot produce and integrate all of the sophisticated components required, many observers argue the MTCR and complementary export controls will probably continue to impede development of the most advanced missiles.

The major ongoing challenge, however, is that much of the international commerce in missiles and missile technology occurs between nations that do not adhere to MTCR guidelines. China and North Korea are not members, although China promised to observe the guidelines after the United States had twice imposed economic sanctions on Chinese companies for transferring missile items to Pakistan, on the condition that the United States would lift those sanctions. North Korea's missile development, production, deployment, and export of missiles has continued largely outside the reach of the MTCR. Reported North Korean exports of missile production technology to Iran, Pakistan, Syria, and Egypt seriously undercut the international standards and goals of the regime. In the view of some analysts, the activities of North Korea demonstrate the failure of the MTCR and the necessity of other measures. Other analysts argue North Korea demonstrates the need to expand the regime in order to make it even more difficult for such missile proliferation to occur.

Some difficulties associated with the nuclear, chemical, and biological nonproliferation regimes may be even more acute with respect to missile technology. The notion of a suppliers' regime dividing the world into "haves" and have-nots" is even more exacerbated in the case of missiles, because there is no treaty and no *quid pro quo* for the have-nots. The International Code of Conduct is an attempt to address this "carrot" side of the carrot-stick equation, but the lack of specificity on incentives is viewed by some as too limited and by others as too potentially expansive. Also, there is a common perception that technology is shared among MTCR members, although the guidelines call for the strong presumption of denial of Category I-class missiles and technology to anyone. The U.S. decision in 2002 to elaborate what constitutes "rare occasions" (wherein Category I presumption of denials could be overruled) lends credence to this view.[80]

---

[80] Testimony given by Vann Van Diepen, Deputy Assistant Secretary of State for Proliferation Controls in a hearing (continued...)

Further, although many of the materials associated with nuclear weapons can be identified and controlled, the materials and components used in missiles are commonly used in a wide range of commercial manufacturing processes. Ballistic missile programs can be nearly indistinguishable from civilian space launch programs, and some missile production equipment, technology, and materials are difficult to distinguish from civilian items. This is particularly acute in the case of UAVs.

As some developing nations become increasingly capable of producing missiles indigenously, the effectiveness of supplier controls may gradually erode. Some analysts see attempts to control missile technology exports as futile and argue for the fewest export restrictions possible, emphasizing the importance to the U.S. economy of exports. Others say the U.S. government should not allow the export of any goods that are likely to harm U.S. national security, despite the potential positive effect on some American business interests.

In addition to the promotion of exports, other foreign policy and national security goals may also compete with missile nonproliferation for government attention and action. For instance, U.S. leaders hope to encourage Russia and China to become stable and responsible actors in their regions and in the international community, to pursue economic and political reforms, and to respect internationally recognized human rights. The United States has sought the cooperation of those two countries and many others in efforts to block nuclear proliferation, terrorism, drug trafficking, and organized crime. Although missile nonproliferation will remain an issue of utmost importance, other goals may occasionally be given greater emphasis. However, when political leaders suspend missile nonproliferation policies in favor of other goals, the credibility of the U.S. policy and that of the MTCR can be damaged, according to many observers. It can become more difficult to persuade other countries to comply with a set of standards when the United States appears to enforce the standards on a selective basis. The priority to be given to missile nonproliferation was occasionally a point of contention between Congress and the Bush Administration.

Congress has established economic sanctions that must be imposed on companies that trade in missile technology contrary to the MTCR guidelines. The imposition, lifting, and waiving of these sanctions frequently cause controversy. Some analysts suggest these negative actions should be coupled with positive incentives to induce countries to refrain from proliferation. Positive incentives could include trade credits, development assistance, military assistance, technology transfers, access to space launch and satellite capabilities, or security guaranties. But other analysts contend the security benefits derived from adhering to the MTCR should be sufficient and that the United States should not try to buy compliance.

According to many foreign policy specialists, the underlying political and security problems that drive proliferation must be resolved before meaningful curbs can be applied to the spread of weapons of mass destruction and missiles. The United States and its partners in the MTCR have helped countries, particularly neighbors in regions of ongoing conflict, adopt confidence-building measures such as those that have contributed to security and cooperation in Europe. Many of these same countries also try to help correct regional imbalances of military forces and to facilitate peace negotiations and arms control talks.

(...continued)

before Senate Government Affairs Committee, Subcommittee on International Security, Proliferation and Federal Services, June 11, 2002.

Security alliances and military assistance also can play a role in restraining missile development. The U.S. security umbrella over Western Europe and parts of Asia and the transfer of large quantities of advanced conventional weapons helped dissuade a number of U.S. allies from developing weapons of mass destruction and helped deter aggression. Some analysts contend that the security of some allies was enhanced by the deterrent power of U.S. nuclear-armed missiles previously deployed in their territory or, possibly in the case of Israel, by indigenous weapons. The U.S. government has also decided that it is appropriate to sell missiles (U.S. Army Tactical Missile Systems) with a potential range of 250 km to countries such as Turkey, Greece, South Korea, Britain, France, and Germany, though it forbids sales of missiles with a range of more than 300 km. However, the superiority of U.S. military technology may actually persuade some adversary countries to develop weapons of mass destruction and missiles as their best means of deterring U.S. intervention.

Some analysts see missile defense systems as a proper alternative to export controls, though most see them as supplementing other military, political, and long-range economic measures (including export controls and sanctions). The United States will likely continue to deploy theater and long-range missile defense systems and has provided such defensive missiles and capabilities to friends and allies in Europe, East Asia, and the Middle East. As the United States seeks to increase defense cooperation in the area of missile defenses, a few have raised issues over the applicability of MTCR guidelines. Additionally, as longer range ballistic missile defense systems are developed, some might question the transfer of such systems or technologies to other countries in the context of the MTCR. For instance, would Chinese development of intermediate-range ballistic missile defense systems be widely viewed as a permitted MTCR export to countries such as Pakistan? Air defense missiles and anti-theater ballistic missiles probably enhance the security of U.S. allies, but none are expected to be 100% effective. In some cases, such as Taiwan, deployments might increase tensions. The Obama Administration and Congress will likely continue to review defense and missile nonproliferation policy objectives in this area.

Appendix A. Proliferation Control Regime Membership

NSG (45)	MTCR (34)	Australia Group (41)
Argentina[a]	Argentina	Argentina
Australia[a]	Australia	Australia
Austria[a]	Austria	Austria
Belarus		
Belgium[a]	Belgium	Belgium
Brazil	Brazil	
Bulgaria[a]	Bulgaria	Bulgaria
Canada[a]	Canada	Canada
China[a]		
Croatia		Croatia
Cyprus[a]		Cyprus
Czech Republic[a]	Czech Republic	Czech Republic
Denmark[a]	Denmark	Denmark
Estonia		Estonia
		European Commission
Finland[a]	Finland	Finland
France[a]	France	France
Germany[a]	Germany	Germany
Greece[a]	Greece	Greece
Hungary[a]	Hungary	Hungary
	Iceland	Iceland
Ireland[a]	Ireland	Ireland
Italy[a]	Italy	Italy
Japan[a]	Japan	Japan
Kazakhstan[a]		
Latvia		Latvia
Lithuania		Lithuania
Luxembourg[a]	Luxembourg	Luxembourg
Malta		Malta
Netherlands[a]	Netherlands	Netherlands
New Zealand	New Zealand	New Zealand
Norway[a]	Norway	Norway
Poland[a]	Poland	Poland
Portugal[a]	Portugal	Portugal

NSG (45)	MTCR (34)	Australia Group (41)
Romania[a]		Romania
Russian Federation[a]	Russian Federation	
Slovakia[a]		Slovakia
Slovenia[a]		Slovenia
South Africa[a]	South Africa	
South Korea[a]	South Korea	South Korea
Spain[a]	Spain	Spain
Sweden[a]	Sweden	Sweden
Switzerland[a]	Switzerland	Switzerland
Turkey[a]	Turkey	Turkey
Ukraine[a]	Ukraine	Ukraine
United Kingdom[a]	United Kingdom	United Kingdom
United States[a]	United States	United States

a.   Zangger member.

Appendix B. Additional Legislation and Executive Orders

Combating Proliferation of Weapons of Mass Destruction Act of 1996, Title VII, Intelligence Authorization Act for Fiscal Year 1997, P.L. 104-293, 50 U.S.C. 2301 note.

National Defense Authorization Act for Fiscal Year 1994, Title XVI, Arms Control Matters, Nonproliferation Provisions, P.L. 103-160.

National Defense Authorization Act for Fiscal Year 1995, Title XV, Arms Control Matters, Nonproliferation Provisions, P.L. 103-337; 22 U.S.C. 2751 note.

Weapons of Mass Destruction Control Act of 1992, Title XV, National Defense Authorization Act for Fiscal Year 1993, P.L. 102-484; 22 U.S.C. 5859a begins at section 1505 of Act.

Antiterrorism and Effective Death Penalty Act of 1996, Title V, Nuclear, Biological, and Chemical Weapons Restrictions, P.L. 104-132, 18 U.S.C. 831 note, and 2331, 42 U.S.C. 262 note, 50 U.S.C. 1522 note.

Arms Control and Nonproliferation Act of 1994, Title VIII, Part A, Foreign Relations Authorization Act, Fiscal Years 1994 and 1995, P.L. 103-236, 22 U.S.C. 2551 note.

Defense Against Weapons of Mass Destruction Act of 1996, Title XIV, National Defense Authorization Act for Fiscal Year 1997, P.L. 104-201, 50 U.S.C. 2301 note.

Foreign Relations Authorization Act, Fiscal Year 2003, Title XI and XIII: Verification of Arms Control and Nonproliferation Agreements, Assistance - P.L. 107-228 (Sec. 1101) 22 USC 2651 note.

Executive Order 13382 (June 28, 2005, 70 FR 38567) Blocking Property of Weapons of Mass Destruction Proliferators and Their Supporters.

Executive Order 13222 (August 17, 2001, 66 FR 44025, August 22, 2001) Continuation of Export Control Regulations, upon the expiration of the Export Administration Act of 1979.

Continued on August 15, 2002 by notice published in Federal Register on August 16, 2002.

Executive Order 13128 (June 25, 1999, 99FR 16634) Implementation of the Chemical Weapons Convention and the Chemical Weapons Convention Implementation Act.

Executive Order 13049 (June 11, 1997, 62 FR 32471) Organization for the Prohibition of Chemical Weapons.

Executive Order 13030 (December 12, 1996, 61 FR 66187) Administration of Foreign Assistance and Arms Exports.

Executive Order 12938 (November 14, 1994, 59 F.R. 59-9, 50 U.S.C. 1701 note) Declares the proliferation of weapons of mass destruction and their means of delivery as an unusual and extraordinary threat and declares a national emergency to deal with that threat.

Amended by EO 13094 (July 28, 1998, 63 FR40803 and by EO 13128 (June 25, 1999, 64 FR 34703).

Executive Order 12946 (January 20, 1995, 60 F.R. 4829, 22 U.S.C. 2551 note) Establishes the President's Advisory Board on Arms Proliferation Policy.

Executive Order 12851 (June 11, 1993, 58 F.R. 33181, 22 U.S.C. 2797 note) Delegates President's authority under the Export Administration Act, Arms Control Export Act, and the Chemical and Biological Weapons Control, Warfare Elimination Act, National Defense Authorization Act for Fiscal Years 1992 and 1993, National Defense Authorization Act for Fiscal Year 1993, and Foreign Relations Authorizations Act for Fiscal Years 1992 and 1993, to the Secretaries of State, Commerce, Defense, and Treasury, and Director of ACDA.

Executive Order 11850 (April 8, 1975, 40 F.R. 16187, 50 U.S.C. 1511 note) Renunciation of certain uses in war of chemical herbicides and riot control agents.

Author Contact Information

Mary Beth Nikitin, Coordinator
Analyst in Nonproliferation
mnikitin@crs.loc.gov, 7-7745

Paul K. Kerr
Analyst in Nonproliferation
pkerr@crs.loc.gov, 7-8693

Steven A. Hildreth
Specialist in Missile Defense
shildreth@crs.loc.gov, 7-7635